MICHAEL N. CUTSUMBIS

A BIBLIOGRAPHIC GUIDE
TO MATERIALS ON GREEKS
IN THE UNITED STATES,
1890 - 1968

Center for Migration Studies — New York

MICHAEL N. CUTSUMBIS

A BIBLIOGRAPHIC GUIDE
TO MATERIALS ON GREEKS
IN THE UNITED STATES,
1890-1968

Center for Migration Studies — New York

MICHAEL N. CUTSUMBIS

A BIBLIOGRAPHICAL GUIDE TO MATERIALS ON GREEKS IN THE UNITED STATES, 1890-1968

ERRATUM

Page 13, line 12: "McSC" should read "MoSC"

Page 92, last line: "Lendis" should read "Leondis"

Page 97, second column, lines 3-4: "... Monastery, 40, 47, 76" should read "...46, 47, 76"

Page 99, second column, line 20: "Parma Seights" should read "Parma Heights"

Page 100, first column: after "Wiest, Walter E., 45" include "Wurdeman, Audrey, 40"

Page 100, second column, line 23: "Miscellaneous Lore ... Detroit" should read "Ethnic Groups in Detroit"

Michael N. Cutsumbis

A BIBLIOGRAPHIC GUIDE ON GREEKS
IN THE UNITED STATES, 1890-1968

CENTER FOR MIGRATION STUDIES
209 Flagg Place
Staten Island, New York 10304

Library of Congress Number 74-130283

FOREWORD

Ethnic groups have been a force affecting the social, political and cultural life of the United States since its beginning. But the last two decades have witnessed a resurgence, sometimes violent, sometimes peaceful, but always forceful, of the ethnic consciousness of the various groups living within the social fabric of the nation. Looking toward the future, America faces the '70's as a decade in which ethnicity will play a major role in its development.

The revival of the ethnic consciousness in the social, political and cultural fields brought about a new academic interest in it. Ethnicicity has been a neglected or repressed field of study in the first half of the present century; since the '50's ethnicity has become one of the major fields of interest in the American academic institutions and social agencies. The history of the ethnic groups is explored through all the existing records with the same passion which was dedicated to the Puritans in the past decades. The knowledge of their past experience becomes instrumental in understanding the present role of the different groups within the national social system.

The Center for Migration Studies presents this ethnic bibliography as a contribution in the general effort to understand the ethnic experience in the United States. A bibliographical guide is primarily an instrument of specialized research. Its usefulness, however, is evident also for anyone who wants to understand either his ethnic background or the experience of other groups which struggled to be included as a functioning subgroup within the American society.

TABLE OF CONTENTS

PREFACE

As part of the study of the "new immigration," scholars have acknowledged, but little studied, the Greek immigration to the United States from 1890-1921. Linguistic inability, unavailability of sources and materials are important in neglecting this subject. Also, neither in numbers nor in influence have the Greeks in the United States played as an important role as some other ethnic groups in the history of the United States. Still the Greeks are a part of the history of American immigration and a part of the people of 20th Century America.

This guide will be useful to scholars concerned with this subject and to others who need to locate works or material on this subject. It is intended that this guide will supplement other bibliographies of the Greeks in the United States, but it is, according to the compiler's knowledge, the most complete selective bibliographic guide to works and materials dealing with the Greeks in the United States from 1890-1968.

This work may be used by many scholars for a variety of purposes. Any criticism, therefore, of each work remains to be done by the user.

INTRODUCTION

This bibliographic guide of works and material dealing with Greeks in the United States from 1890 to 1968, was begun in June, 1967, and completed in December, 1968. It is divided into eleven separate sections. The entries in Sections 1 through 6 are arranged within each part in chronological order. Sections 7 through 11 are arranged in alphabetical order. Most of the number provided in an entry refer to the Library of Congress call number; any other call numbers given, which are not of the Library of Congress, are so indicated with the respective institution assigning the call number.

For works published prior to 1953, the National Union Catalog and the Philadelphia Union Catalog provided locations for almost all the entries listed in this work.

Approximately 99 per cent of the published works was found by using standard reference sources under the subject headings:

"Greeks in the United States"
"Orthodox Eastern Church, Greek"
"Greeks in the U. S."
"Orthodox Eastern Church"

as provided by:

Marguerite V. Quattlebaum, (ed.) *Subject Headings: Used in Catalogs of the Library of Congress.* Seventh Edition. Washington, 1966; Bertha Margaret Frick, *Sears List of Subject Headings.* Eighth Edition. New York, H. W. Wilson Co., 1959, and by consulting previous bibliographies on "Greeks in the United States" in the Library of Congress, in M.A. and Ph.D. dissertations on "Greeks in the United States," and previously published works which contained bibliographies on "Greeks in the United States" and "Immigration."

Approximately 99 per cent of the unpublished works, manuscripts, archdiocesan materials was found in most instances by personally visiting various libraries and by corresponding with all the parishes listed in the 1967-1968 *Greek-Orthodox Yearbook,* by corresponding on the subject with state historical institutions and groups listed in: Christine M. Nuckols, (ed.). *Directory Historical Societies and Agencies in the United States and Canada, 1967-1968.* Nashville, American Association for State and Local History, 1967; National Referral Center for Science and Technology, *A Directory of Information Resources in the United States, Social Sciences*, October 1965, and *Federal Government*, June 1967.

The remaining one per cent of the published and unpublished works in most instances was obtained by communication with others having knowledge of the subject through conversation, correspondence and interview; browsing in related sections of the library stacks; consulting certain fugitive material available to the compiler, e.g. handbills, advertisements, etc.

To stay within manageable bounds, there has been an emphasis on works where the primary subject was on "Greeks in the United States," from 1890-1968; however, some works included treated the aforesaid subject as secondary—it was felt that deletion of such works would limit the usefulness of this bibliographic guide. Works for which no location could be determined have not been included. No published governmental documents have been included.

The format followed throughout, in modified form, is that suggested in: Blanche Prichard McCrum and Helen Dudenbostel Jones, *Bibliographical Procedures and Style.* Washington, 1966; and in A.L.A., *Anglo-American Cataloging Rules*, Chicago, 1967.

ACKNOWLEDGEMENTS

The author wishes to thank the following persons without whom this work would not have been possible:

William T. Alderson, Jr., Editor
American Association for State
  and Local History
Nashville, Tennessee

Dr. Hardee Allen
National Archives
Washington, D.C.

Dr. John Appel
Michigan State University
East Lansing, Michigan

The Reverend Ernest Arambiges
Peoria, Illinois

The Reverend Arthur E. Athans
Dover, New Hampshire

The Reverend John P. Athas
Daytona Beach, Florida

James M. Babcock, Chief
Detroit Public Library
Burton Historical Collection
Detroit, Michigan

The Reverend E. Bardouniotis
Pueblo, Colorado

Allen H. Barton, Director
Bureau of Applied Social Research
New York, New York

The Reverend George N. Bartz
Akron, Ohio 44304

The Reverend Peter G. Bithos
Dallas, Texas

The Reverend Anastasios Blougouras
Detroit, Michigan

The Reverend Emmanuel N.
  Bouyoucas
Baltimore, Maryland

Dr. Edwin C. Buxbaum
University of Delaware
Newark, Delaware

Charlotte Capers
Mississippi State Department of
  Archives and History
Jackson, Mississippi

The Reverend Theodore H. Chelpon
Falls Church, Virginia

Dr. Michael Choukas
Darthmouth College
Hannover, New Hampshire

The Reverend Peter C. Chrisafideis
Baltimore, Maryland

William Coakley
The New York Public Library
New York, New York

The Reverend Evagoras
  Constantinides
Anaheim, California

Everett L. Cooley
Utah State Historical Society
Salt Lake City, Utah

Charles W. Corkran, Director
Texas State Library
Austin, Texas

The Reverend Homer Demopoulos
Seattle, Washington

Christopher B. Devan
The Wilmington Institute Free
  Library and The New Castle
  County Free Library
Wilmington, Delaware

The Reverend George Dimopoulos
Scranton, Pennsylvania

Constantine Divry
New York, New York
The Reverend Constantine N.
  Dombalis
Richmond, Virginia

Arthur Dore
New York, New York

Dr. Kimon Doukas
New York, New York

Walter S. Dunn, Jr.
Buffalo and Erie County
  Historical Soc.
Buffalo, New York

Ardith Emmons, Curator
Swathmore College Peace Collection
Swathmore, Pennsylvania

John Feulner
National Referral Center
Washington, D.C.

Julian J. Gayden, Secretary
Association of North American
  Directory Publishers
Detroit, Michigan

Leo J. Georgiou
Ithaca, New York

Martin K. Gordon
Milwaukee County Historical Society
Milwaukee, Wisconsin

The Reverend Charles Goumenis
Norfolk, Virginia

The Reverend George D. Gregory
Broomall, Pennsylvania

John Tod Hamner
Harris County Historical Society
Houston, Texas

Oscar Handlin, Director
Harvard University
Cambridge, Massachusetts

The Reverend Stanley Harakas
Lexington, Massachusetts

Patricia Harpole
The Minnesota Historical Society
St. Paul, Minnesota

Richard J. Hathaway
State of Michigan Department of
  Education, State Library Division
Lansing, Michigan

Carolyn E. Jakeman
The Houghton Library
Harvard University
Cambridge, Massachusetts

Dr. Nathan M. Kaganoff, Librarian
American Jewish Historical Society
New York, New York

The Reverend Peter Kalellis
Westfield, New Jersey

The Reverend Peter Kastaris
St. Louis, Missouri

The Reverend Steven A. Katsaris
Belmont, California

Dr. James Kiriazis
Youngstown State University
Youngstown, Ohio

The Reverend Frank Kirlangitis
Jacksonville, Florida

The Reverend Basil Kleoudis
Wilmington, North Carolina

Terry Kokas, Archdiocese Officer
New York, New York

Michael N. Kondoleon
Warren, Ohio

The Reverend Arthur K. Kontinos
Arlington, Massachusetts

The Reverend James Kyriakakis
Durham, North Carolina

Judge Gregory Lagakos
Philadelphia, Pennsylvania

The Reverend James J. Laliberte
Tallahassee, Florida

The Reverend Theodore Logothetis
Upper Darby, Pennsylvania

Dr. Gerald MacDonald
New York Public Library
New York, New York

The Reverend Michael Makredes
Kansas City, Missouri

The Reverend Nicholas C. Manikas
Canton, Ohio

The Reverend Chrysostom Maniudakis
Buffalo, New York

9

The Reverend George C. Massouras
South Bend, Indiana

Patrick McGuire, Research Associate
Institute of Texan Cultures
Austin, Texas

The Reverend Dennis Michelis
Warren, Ohio

Neal E. Miller, Director
Wyoming State Archives and
Historical Department
Cheyenne, Wyoming

Mary Molek, Curator
Immigrant Archives
University of Minnesota
Minneapolis, Minnesota

The Reverend Constantine M. Monios
Pittsburgh, Pennsylvania

Charles T. Morrissey, Director
Vermont Historical Society
Montpelier, Vermont

Esther, Moshes
Lancaster, Pennsylvania

The Reverend Spyros Mourikis
Hyannis, Massachusetts

The Reverend Efstathios B. Mylonas
Port Jefferson, L.I., New York

The Reverend Theofanis Nacopoulos
Erie, Pennsylvania

The Reverend George Neofotistos
Denver, Colorado

The Reverend Nikolaos A.
Nikolopoulos
Webster, Massachusetts

Phyllis Nottingham, Librarian
Division of State Libraries
Juneau, Alaska

The Reverend Nicholas G. Paleologos
Hot Springs, Arkansas

The Reverend George C. Pantelis
Knoxville, Tennessee

The Very Reverend George Papadeas
New York, New York

The Reverend Stephen Papadoulias
Springfield, Massachusetts

Dr. John C. Papajohn, Research
Assistant
Brandeis University
Waltham, Massachusetts

C. Papaphotiou
National Herald
New York, New York

The Reverend George T. Pappas
Campbell, Ohio

The Reverend Theotokis N. Pappas
Columbia, South Carolina

The Reverend Thomas J. Paris
Savannah, Georgia

John Patler
Arlington, Virginia

The Reverend Philemon Payiatis
Dayton, Ohio

Panos Peclaris, Archdiocese Officer
New York, New York

R. L. Polk and Company
Detroit, Michigan

The Very Reverend Dr. John
A. Poulos
Long Island City, New York

Georgia Prakis, Archdiocese Officer
New York, New York

Paul Prodromidis
New York, New York

Dr. George Psathas
George Washington University
St. Louis, Missouri

The Reverend Polycarp Rameas
Watertown, New York

Alexandra Routsonis
Salonica, Greece

Dr. Theodore Saloutos
University of California
Los Angeles, California

The Reverend Kallistos Samaras
Chicago, Illinois

The Reverend John P. Sarantos
Lowell, Massachusetts

The Reverend Steven Sarigianis
Bethlehem, Pennsylvania

The Reverend George Scoulas
Pittsburgh, Pennsylvania

The Reverend George Seder
Shreveport, Louisiana

The Reverend Daniel Sfikas
Winston-Salem, North Carolina

Wayne Shirley
Library of Congress
Washington, D.C.

The Reverend Dimitrios Simeonidis
Ogden, Utah 84403

The Reverend Charles J. Simones
New London, Connecticut

Dr. Ellen J. Stekert, Director
Folklore Archives
Wayne State University
Detroit, Michigan

The Reverend Robert G.
Stephanopoulos
Rye, New York

The Very Reverend Eusebius
Stephanou
Fort Wayne, Indiana

The Reverend John T. Tavlarides
Washington, D.C.

Rebecca Tcherikower, Archivist
Yivo Institute for Jewish Research
New York, New York

The Reverend Nicholas G. Terezakis
Trenton, New Jersey

The Reverend Theophilos P.
Theophilos
Los Angeles, California

E. Thompson, Librarian
State Historical Society of Colorado
Denver, Colorado

The Reverend Nicholas C. Trivelas
Charleston, South Carolina

Margaret D. Uridge, Head
General Reference Service
University of California-Berkeley
Berkeley, California

The Reverend Joakim Valasiadis
Freeport, L.I., New York

Barbara Valavanis
Lancaster, Pennsylvania

Leon de Valinger, Jr., State Archivist
State of Delaware Public
    Archives Commission
Dover, Delaware

The Reverend Emmanuel N. Vergis
Milwaukee, Wisconsin

The Reverend Alexander Veronis
Lancaster, Pennsylvania

The Reverend Nicholas L. Vieron
Memphis, Tennessee

Clement G. Vitek, Librarian
The Baltimore Sun
Baltimore, Maryland

The Reverend Carl G. Vouros
New Britain, Connecticut

Mary Whittemore, Data Librarian
International Data Library and
    Reference Service
Berkeley, California

M. Windell
Eleutherian Mills Historical Library
Greenville, Delaware

Edith C. Wise, Reference Librarian
New York University Libraries
New York, New York

This work which would not be complete without thanking The Franklin and Marshall Faculty Research Grant Committee and the staff of the Fackenthal Library, Franklin and Marshall College.

Lancaster, May, 1969   M. N. C.

Marietta, September, 1969

SYMBOLS

AAP	Auburn University, Alabama
AMAU	Air University Library, Maxwell AFB, Alabama
AU	University of Alabama, University, Alabama
AzU	University of Arizona, Tucson, Arizona
CaBVaU	University of British Columbia, Vancouver, B.C.
CL	Los Angeles Public Library, California
CLSU	University of Southern California, Los Angeles, California
CLU	University of California at Los Angeles, California
CoU	University of Colorado, Boulder, Colorado
CSf	San Francisco Public Library, California
CSfM	Mechanics Institute Library, San Francisco, California
CSt	Stanford University Libraries, Stanford, California
CStclu	University of Santa Clara, California
CtHT	Trinity College, Hartford, Connecticut
CtY	Yale University, New Haven, Connecticut
CtY-D	Yale University, Divinity School, New Haven, Connecticut
CU	University of California-Berkeley, California
CU-B	University of California, Bancroft Library, Berkeley, California
DA	U.S. National Agricultural Library, Washington, D.C.
DCU	Catholic University, Washington, DC.
DI	U.S. Department of Interior Library, Washington, D.C.
DLC	U.S. Library of Congress, Washington, D.C.
DPU	Pan American Union Library, Washington, D.C.
DS	U.S. Department of State Library, Washington, D.C.
FTaSU	Florida State University, Tallahassee, Florida
FU	University of Florida, Gainsville, Florida
GEU	Emory University, Georgia
IA	Immigration Archives of University of Minnesota, Minneapolis, Minnesota
IaAs	Iowa State University of Science and Technology, Ames, Iowa
IaU	University of Iowa, Iowa City, Iowa
IC	Chicago Public Library, Illinois
ICHi	Chicago Historical Society
ICJ	John Crerar Library, Chicago, Illinois
ICRL	Center for Research Libraries, Chicago, Illinois
ICU	University of Chicago, Illinois
IEN	Northwestern University, Evanston, Illinois
InU	Indiana University, Bloomington, Indiana
IU	University of Illinois, Urbana, Illinois
KU	University of Kansas, Lawrence, Kansas
KyLx	Lexington Public Library, Kentucky
KyU	University of Kentucky, Lexington
LU	Louisiana State University, Baton Rouge, Louisiana
MB	Boston Public Library, Massachusetts
MBu	Boston University, Massachusetts
MdBe	Enoch Pratt Library, Baltimore, Maryland
MeB	Bowdoin College, Brunswick, Maine
MEU	University of Maine, Orono, Maine
MH	Harvard University, Cambridge, Massachusetts

MH-AH	Harvard University, Andover-Harvard Theological Library, Cambridge, Massachusetts
MHCr	Holy Cross Library, Holy Cross College, Brookline, Mass.
MHCR	Holy Cross Theological School, Brookline, Massachusetts
MH-H	Harvard University, Houghton Library, Cambridge, Mass.
MH-P	Harvard University, Peabody Museum, Cambridge, Mass.
MHW	Harvard University, Widener Library, Cambridge, Mass.
MiD	Detroit Public Library, Michigan
MiDW	Wayne State University, Detroit, Michigan
MiEM	Michigan State University, East Lansing, Michigan
MiU	University of Michigan, Ann Arbor, Michigan
MnU	University of Minnesota, Minneapolis, Minnesota
MnUIA	University of Minnesota, Immigrant Archives, Minneapolis, Minnesota
McSC	Catholic Central Verein of America, St. Louis, Missouri
MoSW	Washington University, St. Louis, Missouri
MoU	University of Missouri, Columbia, Missouri
MsSM	Mississippi State University, State College, Mississippi
MsU	University of Mississippi, University, Mississippi
MWA	American Antiquarian Society, Worcester, Massachusetts
N	New York State Library, Albany, New York
NcD	Duke University, Durham, North Carolina
NcGU	Guilford College, Guilford, North Carolina
NcGW	University of North Carolina at Greensboro, North Carolina
NcRS	North Carolina State of the University of North Carolina at Raleigh, North Carolina
NcU	University of North Carolina, Chapel Hill, North Carolina
NIC	Cornell University, Ithaca, New York
NjP	Princeton University, New Jersey
NjPT	Princeton Theological Seminary, New Jersey
NjR	Rutgers—The State University, New Brunswick, New Jersey
NN	New York Public Library, New York
NNC	Columbia University, New York, New York
NNG	General Theological Seminary of the Protestant Episcopal Church, New York, New York
NNUT	Union Theological Seminary, New York, New York
OBG	Bowling Green State University, Ohio
OC	Public Library of Cincinati and Hamilton County, Ohio
OCl	Cleveland Public Library, Ohio
OClC	Cleveland Clinic Foundation, Ohio
OClL	General Electric Company, Nela Park, Cleveland, Ohio
OClN	General Electric Company, Nela Park, Cleveland, Ohio
OClCS	Case Institute of Technology, Cleveland, Ohio
OCU	University of Cincinnati, Ohio
OClUr	Ursuline College, Cleveland, Ohio
OClW	Western Reserve University, Cleveland, Ohio
OClWHi	Western Reserve Historical Society, Cleveland, Ohio
OEac	East Cleveland Public Library, Ohio
OkU	University of Oklahoma, Norman, Oklahoma
OO	Oberlin College, Ohio
OOxM	Miami University, Oxford, Ohio
Or	Oregon State Library, Salem, Oregon
OrCA	Oregon State University, Corvallis, Oregon
OrU	University of Oregon, Eugene, Oregon

OTU	University of Toledo, Ohio
OU	Ohio State University, Columbus, Ohio
PLB	Lehigh University, Bethlehem, Pennsylvania
PBm	Bryn Mawr College, Pennsylvania
PCarlD	Dickenson College, Carlisle, Pennsylvania
PHC	Haverford College Library, Pennsylvania
PJA	Abington Library Society, Jenkintown, Pennsylvania
PLeB	Bucknell University, Lewisburg, Pennsylvania
PLF	Franklin and Marshall College, Lancaster, Pennsylvania
PLT	Lancaster Theological Seminary, Pennsylvania
PP	Free Library of Philadelphia, Pennsylvania
PPD	Drexel Institute of Technology, Philadelphia, Pennsylvania
PPEB	Eastern Baptist Theological Seminary, Philadelphia, Penn.
PPFr	Friends Free Library of Germantown, Pennsylvania
PPGi	Girard College, Philadelphia, Pennsylvania
PPi	Carnegie Librarie of Pittsburgh, Pennsylvania
PPiU	University of Pittsburgh, Pennsylvania
PPL	Library Company of Philadelphia, Pennsylvania
PPLas	LaSalleCollege, Philadelphia, Pennsylvania
PPLT	Lutheran Theological Seminary, Krauth Library, Philadelphia, Pennsylvania
PPPD	Divinity School of the Protestant Episcopal Church, Philadelphia, Pennsylvania
PPT	Temple University, Philadelphia, Pennsylvania
PPULC	Union Library Catalog of the Philadelphia Metropolitan Area, Pennsylvania
PPV	Van Pelt Library, Philadelphia, Pennsylvania
PPWe	Westminster Theological Seminary, Philadelphia, Pennsylvania
PPWILP	Women's International League for Peace and Freedom % Friends Historical Library, Swarthmore College, Pennsylvania
PSC	Swarthmore College, Pennsylvania
PSt	Pennsylvania State University, University Park, Pennsylvania
PU	University of Pennsylvania, Philadelphia, Pennsylvania
PV	Villanova University, Pennsylvania
PWcT	State College, West Chester, Pennsylvania
RP	Providence Public Library, Rhode Island
RPB	Brown University, Providence, Rhode Island
S	Shippensburg College Library, Shippensburg, Pennsylvania
ScU	University of South Carolina, Columbia, South Carolina
St	State Library, Harrisburg, Pennsylvania
TNJ	Joint University Libraries, Nashville, Tennessee
TU	University of Tennessee, Knoxville, Tennessee
TxDaM	Southern Methodist University, Dallas, Texas
TxU	University of Texas, Austin, Texas
ViBlbV	Virginia Polytechnic Institute, Blacksburg, Virginia
ViU	University of Virginia, Charlottesville, Virginia
WaE	Everett Public Library, Washington
WaT	Tacoma Public Library, Washington
WaU	University of Washington, Seattle, Washington
WHi	State Historical Society, Madison, Wisconsin
WU	University of Wisconsin, Madison, Wisconsin

14

ABBREVIATIONS

(BIF')	In Box... Folder arranged alphabetically by compiler. Box is (12½"x10"x7¼") Amfile, Transfer Cases, Number 710A, and numbered. In possesion of compiler.
BPL	Boston Public Library
ca.	approximately
cf.	Authority for information given
cats.	catalogs or catalog
COP	The Chicago Foreign Language Press Survey. Chicago Public Library Omnibus Project, Works Project Administration, Chicago, Illinois, 1942. 20 p.
diagr.	diagram
(E-)	Envelope (10"x13") with the number of envelope given. In possession of compiler.
(E-OV)	Oversize envelope (11"x14") with the number of envelope given. In possesion of compiler.
exp.	expired
ff.	continued in the work
HC	Holy Cross Library, Holy Cross College, Brookline, Mass.
IA	"Molek, Mary." See item below in unpublished works, p. 50
incl.	includes
illus.	illustration
JBC	John Burton Collection, Detroit Public Library
Micro.	Microfilm
No.	Number
NOM	Newspapers on Microfilm, Washington, D.C., 1967
NYPL	New York Public Library
n.d.	no date given
n.p.	no pagination
passim	here and there in a work
p.	page or pages
ports.	portrait
SIA	Smithsonian Science Information Exchange, Washington, D.C.
st	established
ULS	Union List of Serials, New York, 1965

| Univ. | University Microfilms, P.O. Box 1346 |
| Micro | Ann Arbor, Michigan 48106 |

| v. | volume |

| Wid. | Widener Library, Harvard University |
| WFA | Wayne State Folklore Archives |

WPA-Cop Federal Works Agency Work Projects Administration (Illinois), Bibliography of Foreign Language Newspapers and Periodicals Published in Chicago. Chicago Public Library Omnibus Project, O. P. No. 65-1-54-273(3) Chicago, Illinois, 1942. pp. [i-viii], 61-67.

Yearbook Greek Orthodox Yearbook, see p. 87-88

[ ] Incomplete serial file or information determined by compiler upon examination of material.

? Information incomplete

+ To date or to last date of publication

BOOKS ON GREEKS IN THE UNITED STATES

Maniakēs, Constantinos N. *America and Greece.* Athens, A. Constantinidis, 1899. 41p.
CtY; MiU; MWA; NjP; OO; PU

Lykoudes, Emmanouēl Stylianou. *E Metanastai* [The Immigrants]. Athens, Vasiliki Tipografia Raftanipapa Georgiou, 1903. 81p. Also New York, Ekdotikos Oikos "Prostos," 1919. 61p.
NN; OCU   NYPL-IAG p.v. 121, no. 4

Ghortzis, N. *Ameriki Kai Amerikanoi* [America and Americans]. Athens, 1907.
DLC   E168.G67

Booras, John A. *Ai Ethnikai Thermopylai* [The National Thermopylae]. New York? 1911? 188 p. illus., ports.
DLC; MHW; NN   DF831.B7

Fairchild, Henry Pratt. *Greek Immigration to the United States.* [Introduction by A. G. Keller]. New Haven, Yale University Press, 1911. 278p.
Bibliography, p. 267-270.
DLC; ICJ; MH; MiU; MnU; OCl; OClN; PHC; ViU   JV6824.F3

Burgess, Thomas. *Greeks in America.* Boston, Sherman, French & Company, 1913. 256 p. ports.
Bibliography, p. 235-245.
DLC; MB; MiU; MnUIA; OCl; OClWHi; PBm   E184.G7B9

Demetrios,George. *When I Was a Boy in Greece.* Lathrop, Lee and Shepard, 1913.
DLC; MB; MiU; NN; OCl; OClL; OCiW; OOxM; PJA; PPFr; PPGi

Krikos, Alexandrou. *E Thesis tou Hellinismou en Ameriki* [The Status of Hellenism in America]. Athens, Mblazoudaki Bros., 1915. 233p.
Bibliography, p. 215-221.
DLC; OCl; OCU   E184.G7K9

Casavis, Jack Nicholas. *Kalletes*. New York, Cosmos, 1916. 79 p.
DLC; MHW   DS53.N5C3

Lacey, Thomas James. *A Study of Social Heredity, as Illustrated in the Greek People*. New York, E. S. Gorham, 1916. 76p.
Bibliography, p. 74-76.
Thesis (Ph.D) —New York University, 1915. "List of citations from and references to authorities," p. 69-73.
ICJ; MH; MiU; MnU; NcU; NjP; OCU; OU; PU   DF745.L3

Oikonomidou, Maria (Sarantopoulou). *E Hellines tis Amerikis opos tous Eida* [The Greeks of America as I Saw Them]. New York, D. C. Divry, 1916. 248p. illus., ports.
MH; NN   Wid.-US 10621.15.5

Calodikes, C. S. *The Golden Book, or The Greek and American Spirit*. New York, 1917. 176 p. Also 1923 edition, 256p.
DLC; MHW   AC95.G8C3

Canoutas, Seraphim G. *O Hellinismos En Amerikia* [Hellenism in America]. New York, Kosmos Press, 1918. 334p. illus. ports.
MHW; OC   E184.G7C2

Dendias, Michael A. *Ai Ellinikai Parikoiai ana ton Kosmon* [Greek Colonies Around the World]. Athens, 1919.
MH

Coburn, Frederick. *History of Lowell and Its People*, II. New York, 1920.
MB

Lacey, Thomas James. *Our Greek Immigrants*. New York? 1921? 23p. illus.
DLC; NN   E184.G7L13

Xenides, J. P. *The Greeks in America*. [Introduction by Charles Hatch Sears.] New York, George H. Doran Company, 1922. 160p. incl. map.
Bibliography, p. 154-158.
MnU; OCl; OClW; OU; WaU   E184.G7X3

Anagnostopoulou, Demetrios H. and George. *Mihael Anagnostopoulos*. Athens, 1923.
NN

Kyriakides, Nicholas F. *Ethniki Odeporia eis tin Amerikin, 1918-1919* [Patriotic Mission to America]. Athens, 1924.
MHCR   HC-325.73K

Alessios, Alison B. *The Greek Immigrant and His Reading.* Chicago, American Library Association, 1926. 32p.
Books suggested for library purchase, p. 21-32.
DLC; PPD; PPV; PU   Z711.8.A37

Canoutas, Seraphim. *To Provblema tou Hellinismou tis Amerikis* [The Problem of Hellenism in America]. New York, Herald Printing Syndicate, 1927. 160p.
NN   NYPL-IEE (Greeks)

Asteriou, Asterios. *Ta Hellinika Scholeia en Ameriki* [The Greek Schools in America]. New York, 1931. 84p. ports., table.
NN   NYPL-SSD p.v. 433

Adallis, D. *Thirty-fifth Anniversary: Altoona, Pennsylvania, Greek-American Colony, 1898-1933.* Published by co-operation of the Leading Members of Altoona Greek-American Colony and their Friends. [Altoona, Pa., 1933] 32p. illus., ports. Advertising mater included.
DLC   F159.A5A3

Adallis, D. *Twenty-fifth Anniversary Cumberland, Maryland, Greek-American Colony 1908-1933.* Published by co-operation of the Leading Members of Cumberland Greek-American Colony and their friends. [Cumberland, Md., 1933]. 32p. illus., ports.
DLC   F189.C9A3

——. *Twenty-fifth Anniversary Frederick, Maryland, Greek-American Colony, 1908-1933.* Published by the co-operation of the members of Frederick Greek-American Colony and their friends. [Frederick, Md., 1933?]. 32p. illus., ports., Advertising matter included.
DLC   F189.F8A3

——. *Twenty-fifth Anniversary Fredericksburg, Virginia, Greek Colony 1908-1933.* Published by co-operation of the Leading Members of Fredericksburg Greek-American Colony. [Fredericksburg, Va., 1933]. 32p. illus., ports., Advertising matter included.
DLC   F234.F8A3

———. *Twenty-fifth Anniversary Winchester Greek-American Colony, 1908-1933*. Published by co-operation of the Members of Winchester Greek-American Colony. [Winchester, Va., 1933]. 32p.

DLC   F234.W8A3

———. *Fiftieh Anniversary History of Columbia, South Carolina, Greek-American Colony, 1884-1934*. Published by co-operation of the Leading Members of Columbia Greek-American Colony. [Columbia, S.C., 1934]. 36p. illus., ports., Advertising matter included.

DLC   F279.C7A32

———. *Fiftieth Anniversary Historical Sketch Nashville, Tennessee, Greek Community, 1884-1934*. Published by co-operation of the Leading Members of Nashville Greek Community and their friends. [Nashville, Tenn., 1934]. 16p. illus., ports.

DLC   F444.N2A3

———. *Thirtieth Anniversary History of Knoxville, Tennessee, Greek-American Colony, 1904-1934*. Published by co-operation of the Leading Members of Knoxville Greek-American Colony and their friends. [Knoxville, Tenn., 1934]. 40 p. illus., ports.

DLC   F444.K7A3

———. *Thirtieth Anniversary Historical Brochure of Asheville Greek-American Community*. Published by co-operation of the Leading Members of Asheville Greek-American Community and their friends. [Asheville?, N.C., 1935?]. 44p. illus., ports. Advertising matter included.

DLC   F264.A8A4

———. *Historical Sketch Lexington, Kentucky, Greek Colony, 1909-1935*. Published in co-operation by the Leading Members of Lexington Greek Colony and their friends. [Lexington, Ky., 1935]. 28p. illus., ports.

DLC; MnU   F459.L6A4

———. *Twenty-fifth Anniversary Historical Sketch and Business Guide of Middlesboro and Pineville (Kentucky) Greek-American Colonies, 1910-1935*. Published by co-operation of the Leading Members of the Middlesboro and Pineville Greek-American Colonies and their friends. [Middlesboro? 1935?]. 36p. illus., ports.

DLC   F459.M62A3

————. *Thirtieth Memorial Anniversary Historical and Business Brochure, Greek and Syrian Colonies, Logan, West Virginia.* Published by co-operation of the Leading Members of the Logan Greek and Syrian Colonies and their friends. [Logan, W. Va., 1937]. [44]p. illus. Advertising matter included.
DLC   F249.L6A3

————. *Thirtieth Memorial Anniversary Historical and Business Brochure, Syrian, Greek, American Albanian Colonies of Pikeville, Kentucky, 1937.* Published by co-operation of the Leading Members of the Pikeville Syrian, Greek, American Albanian Colonies and their friends. [Williamson, W. Va., 1937]. [16]p.
DLC   F459.P55A3

————. *Thirtieth Memorial Anniversary Historical and Business Brochure, Greek, Syrian, Armenian Colonies of Williamson, West Virginia.* Sponsored and published in co-operation by the members of the Colonies and their friendly merchants. [Williamson, W. Va., 1937]. 28p. illus., ports.
DLC; NN   F249.W72A3

Valaõras, Vasileos. *Hellenism of the United States.* Athens, P. Leoni Press, 1937. 74p.
Bibliography, 1 p. at end.
DLC; NN   NYPL-IAG p. v. 528

Marshall, Grace E. *Eternal Greece.* Rochester, New York, the DuBois Press, 1938. 214p.
DLC   DF726.M36

Chamberlain, Nicholas. *A Citizen in the Making.* [Akron, Ohio, 1941]. [31]p. illus., ports.
DLC   F499.A3C5

Paleologas, Emmaline Amelia (Milburn). *I Married a Greek.* Mansfield, Ohio, The Stirling Press, 1941. 225p. ports.
DLC   DF726.P27

Marketos, Babēs I. *Hē Hēllas Sto Staurodromi* [Greece at the Crossroads]. New York, National Herald, 1942. 331p. illus. Advertising matter included.
Bibliography, p. 329.
DLC; MHW   D754.G8M3

Warner, W. Lloyd, and Leo Srole. *The Social System of American Ethnic Groups.* Part of *Yankee City Series*, Volume III. New Haven, Yale University Press, 1945. 318p.

Includes: Tables, charts, appendix of distribution of ethnic residences, subject index. One of the important works on Greek Americans although studied only in one community.
PLF

Janetis, Elias. *E Autou Megaliotis, O Metanastis* [His Eminence, the Immigrant]. New York, 1946. 314p. illus.
DLC   PA5655.J3A8

Malafouris, Charalambos. *Hellenes tēs Amerikēs, 1528-1948* [Greeks in America, 1528-1948]. New York, Printed by Isaac Goldman, 1948? 565p. illus., ports. Includes personal ports. and sketches of sponsors, p. 359-552.
Bibliography, p. 553-558.
DLC; MiD   E184.G7M3

Boyd, Rosamonde R. *The Social Adjustment of the Greeks in Spartanburg, South Carolina.* Spartanburg, Williams Printing Company, 1949. 77p.
Bibliography, p. 75-77. A research study completed under a grant from the Carnegie Foundation.
NcD

Economos, Clarence M. *Chronika Palaiochōriou-Kynourias.* 1949. 127p. illus., ports.
NN   NYPL-D-11, 7297

Krikos, Alex. *Hē Metanasteusis* [Immigration]. Athens, 1950. 27p. Summary in English.
DLC   JV8111.K7

Mētropoulos, D. *Greece and Foreign Greeks* [in Greek]. Athens, 1951. 484p.
MH   Wid.-MG1148.951

Triantaphyllidēs, Manolēs. *Hellēnes tēs Amerikēs* [Greeks in America]. Athens, 1952. 96p.
Bibliography, p. 38-39.
DLC; KU; MH; NN   E184.G7T7

Kollias, Sēphēs G. (ed.). *Hellēnikoi Palmoi tōn apodēmōn tēs Amerikēs* [Hellenic Aspirations of those Overseas of America.

The fifty years of D. Callimacho]. New York, 1954. 31p.
DLC   E184.G7K6

Ladogianne, Nina. *Henas Hellinas Stēn Amerikē* [One Greek in America]. Bolos (Volos), 1954. 93p. illus.
DLC   E184.G7L2

Syriōtēs, Geōrgios. *Hē Amerikē Chōris Phantasia* [America Without Illusions]. Athens, Aetos, 1954. 176p.
DLC; MH   E169.1.S99

Theotokas, George. *Dokimio gia ten Amerike* [Essay on America]. Athens, Ikaros, 1954. 236p.
MH   E169.1.T467

Tzatzanēs, Geōrgios A. *The Foreign Greek*. Impressions from a Trip in Europe and America [in Greek]. Piraeus, 1954. 127p. illus.
MH   Wid.-MG1148.954

Zoustis, Basil Th. *O En Ameriki Hellinismos Kai e Drasis Tou-Haistoria Ths Hellinikis Arxiepiskophs Amerikis Boreiou Kai Notiou* [Hellenism in America and Its Activities — The Story of the Greek Archiocese of North and South America]. New York, D. C. Divry, 1954. 414p. ports. Author then "registrar of the Archdiocese."
MH; MB   Wid.-US 10621.65

Androutsopoulos, Grēgorios D. *Skepseis tines Peri Diatērēseōs tou Hellēnismou tēs Amerikēs* [Thoughts (Considerations) Towards the Preservation of Hellenism of America]. Athens, 1955. Summary in English. 18p.
DLC   E184.G7A6

Saloutos, Theodore. *They Remember America: The Story of the Repatriated Greek-Americans*. Berkeley, California University Press, 1956. 153p.
Bibliographical references included in "Notes" (p. 135-142), Bibliography, p. 143-149.
MnU; PP; PPiU; PPULC   E184.G7S3

Stauropoulos, Charalampos P. *Hē Zoē tou Hellēnos stēn Amerikē* [The Life of the Greek in America]. Athens, 1956. 95p. illus.
DLC; MHW   E184.G7S8

Roumanēs, Geōrgios I. *Problems of the Greeks of America* [in Greek]. Athens, 1957. 39p.

MH   Wid.-US10621.12

Ziogas, Elias K. *Ho Hellēnismos tēs Amerikēs; autos ho agnōstes.* [Hellenism in America; That Unknown Factor]. Athens, Hellenic American Publication Agency, 1958. 235p.

MH; OCU   E184.G7Z5

Goulas, Dēmosthenēs Geōrgiou. *Robolaei henas lebentēs* [A Brave Man Hastens]. Athens, 1959. 128p. illus., group ports.

DLC   E184.G7G6

Kotsiphos, Antōnēs. *To Parapono Henos Nekrou Metanastē* [The Grievance of a Dead Immigrant]. London, Canada, 1960. 175p.

DLC   E184.C9K6

Laimos, Geōrgēs Chrēstou. *Dia tēn Epibiōsin tou Apodēmou Hellēnismou* [The Survival of Overseas Hellenism]. London, [196-] 22p.

DLC, MHW   E184.G7D5

Papoulias, Angelos. *Anamnisis Apo Ti Zoi Tou Ellinismou Tis Kalifornias* [Recollections (or Memoirs) of Greek Life of California]. [San Francisco, California, 1960] 350p. illus.

CSf; MH   Wid.-US10621.37

Frantsis, George Th. *Strangers at Ithaca: The Story of the Spongers of Tarpon Springs.* St. Petersburg, Florida, Great Outdoors Publishing Company, 1962. 240p.

Bibliography included.

FTaSU

Kollias, Sēphēs G. *Dēm. Kallimachos.* Athens, 1963. 91p. ports.

Bibliography, p. 25-26. "Works of D. Kallimachos", p. 27-30.

DLC   E184.G7K58

Kontargyres, Theodoros N. *Ho Apodemos Hellenismos Ths Amerikes* [The Overseas Greek of America]. Athens, 1964. 200p.

Bibliography, p. 197-200.

DLC   E184.G7K7

Manos, Charles S. *Hē Zōē Henos Matanastē* [The Life of an Immigrant]. Athens, 1964. 238p. illus., port.

DLC; MH   E184.G7M34

Papas, Arēs. *The Personality of the Greek American* [in Greek]. Athens, 1964. 194p. illus.
Thesis (Ph.D.) — Athens
MH   Wid.-US 10621.36

Saloutos, Theodore. *The Greeks in the United States*. Cambridge, Harvard University Press, 1964. 445p. illus., ports.
Bibliography, p. 389-400. The standard historical work in English on the Greeks in the United States up to 1962.
DLC; MH; MnU; MoSW; NjR; NN   E184.G7S29

Alexopoulos, Angelos N. *Duo Kosmoi Dokimia* [Two Worlds, 40 Essays in Greek and English]. Athens, 1966. 231p.
NN   NYPL-D16,1894

Vlachos, Evangelos C. *An Annotated Bibliography of Greek Migration*. Athens, Social Sciences Centre [Superceded by National Centre of Social Researches], 1966. 127p. (Mimeographed).
PLF(E-83)

———. *The Assimilation of Greeks in the United States*. Athens, National Centre of Social Researches, 1968. 200p.
PLF(E-83)

Saloutos, Theodore. *The Greeks in America; A Student's Guide to Localized History*. New York, Teachers College Press, 1967. 36p.
Bibliographies included.
DLC; IC   E184.G7S28

ARTICLES ON GREEKS IN THE UNITED STATES

Holbrook, Agnes Sinclair. "Map Notes and Comments," in Jane Addams (ed.), *Hull House Maps and Papers: A Presentation of Nationalities and Wages in a Congested District of Chicago*, by Residents of Hull House—a social settlement at 335 South Halstead Street, Chicago, Illinois. Boston, Thomas Y. Crowell and Company, 1895. pp. 3-23. Includes Department of Labor (1893) Tenement and Family Schedules and Nationality and Wage Maps.
PLF (BIF); PPWILP   HV 4196, C4H7, 1895

Anonymous. "Life Story of a Pushcart Peddler," *Independent*, LX (February 1, 1906), 274-279.
CSt; MH; NN; NNC; PLF

Abbott, Grace. "Study of the Greeks in Chicago," *American Journal of Sociology*, XV (November 1909), 379-393. 12 notes including 6 tables with sources given.
CSt; MH; NN; NNC; OCU; PLF

Fairchild, H. P. "Causes of Emigration from Greece," *Yale Review*, XVIII (August 1909), 176-196. 16 notes, 5 tables.
DLC; NN; NNC

Vlachou, Andrew. "Peri tou en Ameriki Ellinismou apo Emporikis, Koinonikis kai Ethnikis Apopseos" (Regarding Hellenism in America from a Commercial, Social, and National Viewpoint), *Hellinismos*, XII (May 1909), 271-283.
OCU; PLF (BIF)

Weyl, W. E. "Pericles of Smyrna and New York," *Outlook*, XCIV (February 26, 1910), 463-472.
CSt; DLC; MB; NN; NNC; PLF

Cooke, T. S. "The Greeks in the United States," *Eastern and Western Review*. Boston, November 1910.
DLC; MB

Hunt, Milton B. "The Housing of Non-Family Groups of Men in Chicago," *American Journal of Sociology*, XVI (1910), 145-171. 13 notes.
CSt; DCU; MH; NN; NNC; PLF

Lauck, W. Jett. "Industrial Communities," *The Survey*, XXV (January 7, 1911), 579-586.
CSt; DLC; MH; NN; NNC; PLF

Terhune, L. B. "Greek Bootblack," *Survey*, XXVI (September 16, 1911), 852-854.
CSt; DLC; MH; NN; NNC; PLF

Anonymous. "As the Alien Sees Himself," *Independent*, LXXV (August 28, 1913), 478-479. An editorial.
CSt; DLC; MH; NN; NNC; PLF

Sills, K. C. M. "Greek-Americans," *Nation*, XCVII (October 2, 1913), 309.
CSt; DLC; MH; NN; NNC; PLF

Wells, R. R. "American Hellenes," *Nation*, XCIX (July 23, 1914), 102.
CSt; DLC; MH; NN; NNC; PLF

Walker, Natalie. "Chicago Housing Conditions. Greeks and Italians in the Neighborhood of Hull House," *American Journal of Sociology*, XXI (November 1915), No. 3, 285-316. 19 notes.
CSt; DLC; MH; NN; NNC; PLF

Anonymous. "America's Vest-Pocket Athens," *Literary Digest*, LIV (March 17, 1917), 743-744.
CSt; DLC; MH; NN; NNC; PLF

United States Bureau of Education. "Greeks in America," *Literary Digest*, LIX (December 7, 1918), 37. Prepared for *Literary Digest* by United States Bureau of Education.
CSt; DLC; MH; NN; NNC; PLF

Cassavetis, N. J. "L'Avenir de L'Hellénisme D'Amérique," *Etudes Franco-Grecques*, Paris, 1920, *Année* 3, 86-100.
DLC; NN

Roberts, K. L. "They Sometimes Come Back," *Saturday Evening Post*, CXCIV (September 10, 1921), 12-13.
CSt; DLC; MH; NN; NNC; PLF

Alessios, Alison B. "Selection and Purchase of Modern Greek Books," *The Library Journal,* XLVII (January-December 1922), 866.
CSt; DLC; MH; NN; NNC; PLF

Quigley, M. "Greek Immigrant and the Library," *Library Journal,* XLVII (October 15, 1922), 863-865.
CSt; DLC; MH; NN; NNC; PLF

Mears, E. G. "Unique Position in Greek Trade of Emigrant Remittances," *Quarterly Journal of Economics,* XXXVII (May 1923), 535-540. 5 notes.
CSt; DLC; MH; NN; NNC; PLF

Lontos, S. S. "American Greek," *American Speech,* I (1926), 307-310.
S

Polyzoides, Adamantios Th. "What the Greeks Think of America," *Travel,* XLVII (October 1926), 20-23.
CL; CLU; DLC; OU; PP; PPi

Fairchild, Henry Pratt. "The Greeks," in *Immigrant Backgrounds,* Henry Pratt Fairchild (ed.), New York, John Wiley and Sons, 1927, p. 58-70. Bibliography, p. 70.
PHC; PP; PPLas; PPT; PU

Christowe, Stoyan. "Kyotchek," *Outlook,* CLV, No. 2 (May 14, 1930), 48-49, 74-75.
DLC; MH; NN; NNC; PLF

Lagoudakis, Charilaos. "Greece and Michigan," *Colonial Review,* (April, March 31, 1930).
MiD   JBC—E&M, 7404, 325.2495

Lagoudakis, Charilaos. "Greeks in Michigan," *Michigan History Magazine,* XIV (1930), 15-27. 35 notes.
CSt; DLC; MH; NN; NNC; St

Vlachou, Andrew. "O en Ameriki Hellinismos" (Hellenism in America), *Hellinismos,* XXXIII (February 1930), 90-106.
OCU; PLF (BIF)

Nouarou, G. M. "Hellino-Amerikanikai Scheseis" (Greek-American Relations), *Hellenismos,* XXXIV (December 1931), 742-751.
OCU; PLF (BIF)

Anonymous. "Marrying the Adriatic in Florida," *Golden Book,* XVI (November 1932), Sup. 16a.
PLF

Fordyce, Wellington G. "Immigrant Colonies in Cleveland," *Ohio Archeological and Historical Quarterly,* XLV (1936), 320-340. 49 notes.
CSt; DLC; NN; NNC; PLF (BIF); PU; MH

Fordyce, Wellington G. "Immigrant Institutions in Cleveland," *Ohio State Archeological and Historical Quarterly,* (October 1936, April 1937, April 1938). 51 notes.
CSt; DLC; MH; NN; NNC; PLF (BIF); PU

Lee, Dorothy Demetracopoulou. "Folklore of the Greeks in America," *Folk-Lore,* XLVII (1936), 294-310.
CSt; DLC; MH; NNC; OC

Smith, Mapheus. "National Origins of Prominent Immigrants," *Sociology and Social Research,* XX (May, June 1936), 422-432. 8 notes.
CSt; DLC; MH; NN; NNC; PLF

Choukas, Michael. "Greek Americans," in *Our Racial and National Minorities,* Francis J. Brown and Joseph Slabey Roucek (eds.). New York, Prentice-Hall 1937. pp. 339-357. 17 notes.
DLC; NcD; NcRS; OCl; OClW; OU; PBm; PHC; PPT; PU
E184.A1B8

Anonymous. "My Heritage," *Atlantic,* CLXII (December 1938), 846-847.
CSt; MH; NN; NNC; PLF

Ellis, Leonora B. "Harvest of the Sea Floor—Sponge Gathering by the Largest Unmixed Greek Community in America," *Natural History,* XLI (January 1938), 62-66.
PLF

Doering, Eileen Elita. "A Charm of the Gulf of Mexico Sponge Fishers," *Journal of American Folklore,* LII (1939), 123.
CSt; MH-P; MB; NN; NNC

Rankin, Lois. "Detroit Nationality Groups," *Michigan Historical Magazine,* XXIII, No. 2 (Spring number, 1939), 140-146.
MiD
JBC-F561.M57, v. 23

Adamic, Louis. "Greeks Came to Tarpon Springs," in *From Many Lands,* Louis Adamic (ed.), Harper and Brothers, 1940. pp. 116-131.
PLF; PP; PPD; PPEB; PPiU; PPT; PSC; PWcT   E184.A1A3

Brown, Carroll N. "Shall the Children of Greek Americans Learn Greek?" *Hellenic Spectator,* I, No. 3 (May 1940), 3-4.
NN

Loukas, Christ. "Effective Greek Schools, A Program," *Hellenic Spectator,* I, No. 5 (July 1940), 3-4.
NN

Loukas, Christ. "Status of Greek Population in the United States," *The Hellenic Spectator,* I, No. 1 (February 1940), 3-9.
NN

Hellenic Spectator. "Greek Schools," *Hellenic Spectator,* by the Editor, (March 1940), 5-6.
NN

Adamic, Louis. "Greece and Greek Americans," in *Two Way Passage,* Louis Adamic (ed.), New York, Harper and Brothers, 1941. pp. 144-148.
PLF   E184.A1A33

Adamic, Louis. "Greek Immigration in United States: What They Do, What They Contribute, What They Think," *Commonweal,* XXXIII (January 31, 1941), 366-368.
CSt; DLC; MH; NN; NNC   AP2.06897, v. 33

Binsse, H. L. "Mr. Phasoulias; Eating in Greek Restaurants," *Commonweal,* XXXIII (January 31, 1941), 372-373.
CSt; DLC; MH; NN; NNC

Hartley, H. "Greek Way: Sponge Divers of Tarpon Springs," *Colliers,* CVII (May 17, 1941), 18-19.
CSt; DLC; MH; NN

Corse, Carita, and the Florida Writers Project. "Greek-Americans of Florida," *Athene,* III (1942), No. 5, 17-21; No. 6, 22-25, 29; No. 7, 22-26; No. 8, 10-12, 15; No. 9, 10-12; No. 10, 14-15; IV 1943), No. 2, 12-13; No. 3, 10-11, 13.
DLC; NNC

Key, A. "Treasure on the Ocean Floor; Greek Divers Make Tarpon Springs the Sponge Port of the Earth," *Saturday Evening Post,* CCXIV (June 20, 1942), 12-13ff. illus.
CSt; DLC; MH; NN; NNC

Lee, D. Demetracopoulou. "Greek Accounts of Vrykalakas," *Journal of American Folklore,* LV (1942), 126-132.
CSt; MH-P; NN; NNC; PLF

Balk, Helen H. "Economic Contributions of the Greeks to the United States," *Economic Geography,* XIX (1943), 270-275. Tables, Maps.
MU; PLF; St; S

Doering, J. Frederick. "Folk Customs and Beliefs of Greek Sponge Fishers of Florida," *Southern Folklore Quarterly,* VII (June 1943), 105-107. 2 notes.
CL; DLC; NNC; PLF

Adamic, Louis. "Americans from Greece," *Woman's Day,* VII, No. 10 (July 1944), 22ff.
DLC; NN

Constant, Theodore N. "Racial Prejudice and the Greek Stock in the United States," *Athene,* V (Autumn 1944), 8-11. 15 notes.
DLC; NNC

Wessel, Bessie B. "The Ethnic Survey of New London, Connecticut, 1938-1944," *American Journal of Sociology,* L (September 1944), 85-98.
CSt; DCU; MH; NN; NNC; PLF

Bossard, James H. S. "The Bilingual as a Person—Linguistic Identification with Status," *American Sociological Review,* X (December 1945), 699-709. 8 notes.
DLC; NN; NNC; PLF

Constant, Theodore N. "Employment and Business of the Greeks in the United States," *Athene,* VI (Winter 1945), 37-39; VII (Summer 1946), 40-41; VII (Autumn 1946), 28-29; VII (Winter 1947), 37-41, 46. 13 notes.
DLC; NNC

Adamic, Louis. "Americans from Greece," *Nation of Nations*, Louis Adamic (ed.), New York, Harper and Brothers, 1945. pp. 266-286. 4 notes, p. 361.
PLF   E184.A1A32

Politis, M. J. "Greek-Americans," in *One America*, Francis J. Brown and Joseph Slabey Roucek (eds.), New York, Prentice Hall, 1945, revised edition. pp. 242-257. 15 notes.
DI; DPU; OClUr; PBL; PP; PPEB; PSt; ViU

Saloutos, Theodore. "The Greeks in the United States," *South Atlantic Quarterly*, XLIV (January 1945), 69-81. Reprinted in: *Fifty Years of the South Atlantic Quarterly*, Durham, 1952. pp. 396-18.
CSt; DLC; MH; NN; NNC; PLF; PPi

Lee, Dorothy Demetracopoulou. "Greek Tales of Nastradi Hodjas," *Folklore*, LVII (1946), 188-195.
CSt; DLC; MH; NN; NNC; PLF

Constant, Theodore N. "Greek Immigration and Its Causes," *Athene*, VIII (Spring 1947), 21-24. 23 notes.
DLC; NNC; PCarlD

Covert, Alice Lent. "Chronicle of Americanization," *Reader's Digest*, L (February 1947), 51-54.
CSt; DLC; MH; NNC; PLF

Green, Arnold W. "A Re-examination of the Marginal Man Concept," *Social Forces*, XXVI, No. 2 (December 1947), 167-171. 19 notes.
CSt; DLC; MH; NN; NNC; PLF

Harris, Jennie E. "Sponge Fishermen of Tarpon Springs," *National Geographic Magazine*, XCI (January 1947), 119-136.
CSt; DLC; MH; NNC; PLF

Lee, Dorothy Demetracopoulou. "Greek Tales of Priests and Priestwife," *Journal of American Folklore*, LX (1947), 163-167.
CSt; MH-P; NN; NNC; PLF

Loomis, Stuart D., and Arnold W. Green. "The Pattern of Mental Conflict in a Typical State University," *Journal of Abnormal and Social Psychology*, XLII, No. 3 (July 1947), 342-355. 12 notes.
CSt; MH; NN; NNC; PLF

Papanikolas, Helen Zeese. "The Fortress and the Prison," *Utah Humanities Review*, I, No. 2 (1947), 134-146.
CLU; MH; NN; NNC

Constant, Theodore N. "Life of Earlier Greek Immigrants in the United States," *Athene*, VIII (Winter 1948), 26-29. 5 notes.
DLC; NNC; PCarlD

Lawren, J. "The Sponge Capital of America," *Travel*, XCI, No. 1 (May 1948), 23-25, 34.
CL; CLU; CSf; DLC; MB; NNC; OU; PP; PPi

Montgomery, Margaret. "A Macedonian Wedding in Indianapolis," *Hoosier Folklore*, VII (1948), 101-104.
NcU; PLF

Nelson, Lowry. "Speaking of Tongues," *American Journal of Sociology*, LIV (November 1948), 202-10. 9 notes.
CSt; DCU; MH; NN; NNC; PLF

Stycos, Mayone J. "The Spartan Greeks of Bridgetown: Community Cohesion," *Common Ground*, VIII (Spring 1948), 24-34; (Summer 1948), 72-86; (Winter 1948), 61-70.
CL; DLC; MB; NN; NNC

Chyz, Yaroslav, and Read Lewis. "Agencies Organized by Nationality Groups in the United States," *Annals, American Academy of Political and Social Science*, CCLXII (March 1949), 148-158.
CSt; DLC; MH; NN; NNC; PLF

Matthews, Ernest S. "Merry Greek Tales from Buffalo," *New York Folklore Quarterly*, V (1949), 268-275.
CSt; DLC; MB; NN; NNC; PLF

Treudley, Mary B. "Former Organization and the Americanization Process, with Special Reference to the Greeks of Boston," *American Sociological Review*, XIV (February 1949), 44-53. 8 notes.
PLF

Anonymous. "The Forgotten Generation," *Athene*, X (Winter 1950), 22-23, 41-42.
DLC; NNC; PCarlD

Constant, Theodore N. "Greek-American Colonies, Churches and Schools in the United States," *Athene*, XI (Autumn 1950), 26-27; XI (Winter 1951), 22-23, 54; XII (Spring 1951), 34-35, 50. 10 notes.
DLC; NNC; PCarlD

Doukas, Kimon. "The Story of Ahepa," *Athene*, XI (Summer 1950), 39-43.
DLC; NNC; PCarlD

Rozakos, N. "E Protoi Lacedaimonoi Metanastes stin Ameriki" (The First Spartan Immigrants in America), *Nea Estia*, XLVIII (August 15, 1950), 1080-1084.
IEN

Constant, Theodore N. Hellenic Bar Association, Chicago Symposium, "Problems of Greek-Americans," *Athene*, XII, No. 3, 29-30, 60-64; XII, No. 4, 22-24; XIII, No. 1, 28-29, 56-58. *Note*: Vols. 12 and 13 bound together, 1951-53.
DLC; NNC

Lee, Dorothy Demetracopoulou. "Greek Personal Anecdotes of the Supernatural," *Journal of American Folklore*, LXIV (1951), 307-312. Gives nativity of informants.
CSt; MH-P; NN; NNC; PLF

Lee, Dorothy Demetracopoulou. "Three Romances from Pontos," *Folklore*, LXII (1951), 388-397, 449-453.
CSt; MH; NN; NNC

Vlavianos, B. J. "Greek Americans," in *One America*, Francis James Brown and Joseph Slabey Roucek (eds.), New York, Prentice Hall, 1952, third edition, pp. 239-244. 6 notes.
PV   E184.A1B87

Nichols, Priscilla M. "Greek Lore from Syracuse, New York," *New York Folklore Quarterly*, IX (1953), 109-117.
CSt; DLC; MB; NN; NNC; PLF

Triantaphyllidēs, Manolēs. "The Greek of Greek Americans," [in Greek] Thessaloniki, 1953. Reprint from "HELLINIKA," XII, 302-331.
MH

Papanikolas, Helen Zeese. "The Greeks of Carbon County," *Utah Historical Quarterly*, Salt Lake City, XXII, No. 2 (April 1954), 143-164.
Bibliographical notes.
CSt; MH; NN; NNC

Anonymous. "America," *Look*, (May 31, 1955), 34-39.
S

Katsanevas, Mike. "Happiness as an Import," *Life*, XXXVIII January 10, 1955), 26-27. illus.
PLF

Maisel, Albert Q. "The Greeks Among Us," *Reader's Digest*, LXVII (July 1955), 113-118.
PLF

Alatis, James E. "The Americanization of Greek Names," *Names* (September 1955), 137-156.
CSt; DCU; OCU; P; PPiD; PSt; PLF (BIF)

Rozakos, N. I. "Greek Social Groups in America," *Krikos*, VI, No. 59-60 (1955), 70-71.
MH; PLF(BIF)

Hamilton, A. "Family Reunion, U.S.A.," *Reader's Digest*, LXVIII (March 1956), 189-190ff.
CSt; DLC; MH; NNC; PLF

Dorson, Richard M. "Tales of a Greek-American Family on Tape," *Fabula*, I (1957), 114-143. Transcriptions of tapes, 119-141. Appendix to tape recording, 141-143.
DLC; MU

Macris, James. "Changes in Lexicon of New York City Greek," *American Speech*, XXXII, No. 2 (May 1957), 102-109. 27 notes.
PLF

Notopoulos, Dēmetrios A. "Tragoudia Dodekanēsion Tēs Amerikēs" (Dodecanesian Songs of America), in *Laographia*, Athens, 26 cm. *Tomos* 17 (1957), 22-29.
CSt; ICU; MH; NN

Giannakoulis, Theodore. "Eisagoge sten Historia ton Hellinoamerikanon" (Introduction to the History of Greek-Americans), *Argonautes*, A (1959), 167-177.
NN

Hole, Jonathan A. "Greek Community in Reading (Pennsylvania), Berks County," *Historical Review of Berks County*, XXIV, No. 1 (Winter 1958-59), 17-30.
PLF (E-22).

Kallimachos, Demetrios. "Greek College in America," *Argonautes*, A (1959), 43-48. 3 notes.
NN

Loures, N. "He Metanasteuses sten Amerike kai ta Apotelesmata tes gia ten Hellada" (Immigration to America and Its Results for Greece), *Argonautes*, A (1959), 178-185. 7 notes.
NN

Rosen, Bernard C. "Race, Ethnicity, and the Achievement Syndrome," *American Sociological Review*, XXIV (1959), 47-60. 28 notes.
DLC; NN; NNC; PLF

Saloutos, Theodore. "Ai Antipossis mou peri Helleno-Amerikanon" (My Impressions about Greek-Americans), *Argonautes*, A (1959), 120-127.
NN

Agapitidis, Sotirios. "Emigration from Greece," *Migration*, I (January-March 1961), 53-61. 1 table.
MiD; PLF(BIF)

Lauquier, Helen Capanidou. "Cultural Change Among Three Generations of Greeks," *American Catholic Sociological Review*, XXII (1961), 223-232. 71 notes.
CStclu; DLC; MH; NN

Georges, Robert A. "Greek Folk Remedy in America," *Southern Folklore Quarterly*, XXVI (June 1962), 122-126. 6 notes.
CL; DLC; NNC; PLF

Georges, Robert A. "Matiasma: Living Folk Belief," *Midwest Folklore*, III (1962), 69-74. 31 notes including list of informants.
CLU; DLC; MEU; PLF

Georges, Robert A. "The Greeks of Tarpon Springs: An American Folk Group," *Southern Folklore Quarterly*, XXIX, No. 2 (June 1965), 129-141. 17 notes.
CL; DLC; NNC; PLF

Fay, Sharon E. "Greek Community: Strong Ties, but No Ghetto," in *Los Angeles Times*, Tuesday, January 28, 1969 — Part IV, p. 1, 2 (col. 1). Two parts.

Clipping sent to compiler by Theodora D. Argue, St. Katharine Greek Orthodox [Church] Ladies Philoptochos Society, Redondo Beach, California. Typed letter included with clipping dated January 28, 1969, to compiler signed by Theodora D. Argue, Redondo Beach, giving additional information on parishioners of St. Katherine Church, Redondo Beach [Los Angeles].

PLF(E-70)

GREEK-AMERICANS IN FICTION

Adams, Samuel Hopkins. "Orpheus, Who Made Music in Our Square," *Our Square and the People in It*, Boston, Houghton Mifflin, 1917.
AzU; LU; MiU; NcU; ViU   PZ3.A2170u

Dobie, Charles Caldwell. "All or Nothing," *Arrested Moment and Other Stories*, New York, John Day Company, 1927.
DLC; MB; NcD; NN; ViU

Michalaros, Demetrios Antonio. *The Legend of America* (1927).
MH

——. *Sonnets of An Immigrant* (1930).
IEN

Farrell, James T. "Benefits of American Life," *Guillotine Party and Other Stories*, New York, Vanguard Press, 1935.
DLC; NjP

Geannopulos, James Nicholas. *Mother's Wish*. St. Louis, 1936.
DLC

Saroyan, William. "Only Guy in Town," *Little Children*, New York, Harcourt, Brace and Company, 1937.
OClW; OEac; PPL; PU; ViU

Rhodokamakes, Konstantinos P. *Forever Ulysses*. New York, The Viking Press, 1938.
NcD; OCU; OO; OU; PBm; PSC; PPT; TxU; ViU

Limberis, Dean [pseud.]. "Kids Think Fast, A Story," *Hellenic Spectator* (March 1940), 6-7.
NN

Newhouse, Edward. "Manny Hirsch," *Anything Can Happen*, New York, Harcourt, Brace and Company, 1941.
DLC

Kerr, Annie Barclay. "Little House for God," *Strangers No Longer,* New York, Friendship Press, 1943.
DLC; OO   PZ3.K4602St

Zirpiades, Fotine. "Portrait of Papa," *Common Ground,* IV (Autumn 1943), 80-85.
CLU; DLC; MB; NNC; PLeB

Zirpiades, Fotine. "Sophia Becomes an American," *Common Ground,* IV (Winter, 1943), 97-102.
CLU; DLC; MB; NNC; PLeB

Drickamer, Jewel Annette. "Heart's Tongue," *Common Ground,* V, No. 1 (1944), 80-81.
CLU; DLC; MB; NNC

Freund, Philip. "Young Greek and the Creole," *Young Greek and the Creole and Other Stories,* New York, Pilgrim House, 1944.
DLC; NcD; PP; ViU

Kantor, MacKinley. "That Greek Dog," *Author's Choice,* New York, Coward-McCann Publishing Corporation, 1944.
MiU; NcD; OCl; OClCS; OOxM; OrT; TxU

Vardoulakis, Mary. *Gold in the Streets.* New York, Dodd, Mead & Company, 1945.
NcD; NcGU; OCl; OO; PHC; PP; TxU   PZ3.V3987G0

Grossberg, Elmer. *Farewell, My Son.* New York, Julian Messner & Company, 1946.
CoU; DLC   PZ3.G9137Far

Demetrios, George. *When Greek Meets Greek.* Boston, Houghton Mifflin, 1947.
FTaSU; LU; N; OClC   DF741.D4

Kamal, Ahmad. *Full Fathom Five* [1st edition]). Garden City, New York, Doubleday, 1948.
CU; MH   PZ3.K128Fu

Bezzerides, Albert Isaac. *Thieves Market.* New York, Charles Scribner's and Sons, 1949.
OEac; PSt   PZ3.B46976Tj

Foster, Joseph O'Kane. "I Gotta Teach Her Some English," *Common Ground,* IX, No. 3 (1949), 32-34.
CLU; DLC; MB; NNC

Auslander, Joseph, and Audrey Wurdeman. *The Islanders*. New York, Longmans, Green and Company, 1951. 305p.

KyLx; MB; Or; PP; PPULC; PU; ViU   PZ3.A929Is

Cotsakis, Roxane. *Wing and the Thorn*. Atlanta, Tupper and Love, 1952.

CoU; NN   PZ4.C846Wi

Brace, Gerald Warner. *Bell's Landing*. New York, Norton, 1955. 333p.

NcD; OCU; OO; OO; OOxM; PPL; PU   PZ3.B7217Be

Athas, Daphne. *The Fourth World*. New York, Putnam, 1956. 318p.

CU; IU; MiU; NcGW; Or; TxU; ViU; WaE

Thompson, Ariadne, *Octagonal Heart*. Indianapolis, Bobbs-Merrill, 1956. 221p.

CU; IU; NcGW; NN; OCl; PP; TxU; ViU; WaT; WaU

       PZ4.T4660c

Chamales, Tom T. *Never So Few*. New York, Scribners and Sons, 1957. 499p. illus. World War, 1939-1945 Fiction.

AAP; AMAU; CtY; CU; FTaSU; IaAS; IU; LU; MH; NcD; NIC; OCl; OkU; PP; ScU; TxU; ViU; WaU

Myrer, Anton. *The Big War*. New York, Appleton-Century-Crofts, 1957. 463p.

AMAU; AU CaBVaU; CtU; CU; FU; IU; KyU; LU; MH; MiU; MnU MsSM; NNC; OCL; OU; PP; TU; TxU

Sourian, Peter. *Miri*. New York, Pantheon, 1957. 219p.

CSt; CU; GEU; LU; MH; MiU; MnU; NIC; NN; ScU; TxU; WaU

       PZ4.S724Mi

Chamales, Tom T. *Go Naked in the World*. New York, Charles Scribner's Sons, 1959. 461p.

MoU; NIC; NjP; OCl; ScU; TNJ; TxU   PZ4.C439Go

Dilles, Jim. *The Good Thief*. New York, Thomas Y. Crowell and Company, 1959. 251p.

WU

Petrakis, Harry Mark. *Lion at My Heart*. Boston, Little, Brown & Company, 1959. 238p.

CtY; FU; IaU; ICU; IU; KU; MH; MnU; NIC; NjP; NN; OCl; OTU; PP; RP; RPB; TxU; ViU; WU   PZ4.P4885LiZ

Kazan, Elia. *America, America.* [Introduction by S. N. Behrman]. New York, Stein and Day, 1962. 190p.

DLC; CtY; ICU; IEN; MH; MiU; MsU; NjP; NNC; NRU; OCl; RP; RPB PZ4.K238Am

Brelis, Dean. *My New Found Land.* Boston, Houghton Mifflin, 1963. 209p.

DLC; MoSW; OClW PZ4.B835My

Christy, George. *All I Could See From Where I Stood.* Indianapolis, Bobbs-Merrill Company, Inc., 1963. 220p.

DLC; ViBlbV

Doulis, Thomas. *Path For Our Valor.* New York, Simon and Schuster, 1963. 384p.

ViBlbV

Petrakis, Harry Mark. *The Odyssey of Kostas Volakis.* New York, David McKay Company, Inc., 1963. 271p.

CtY; DLC; NN PZ4.P48850d

Thompson, Ariadne. "Our Octagonal World," *Reader's Digest,* LXXXII (May 1963), 279-299.

CLU; DLC; MH; NNC

Kimbrough, Emily. "Koula; Excerpt from Forever Old, Forever New," *Ladies Home Journal,* LXXXI (November 1964), 87ff. illus.

CSfM; DLC; NN

Petrakis, Harry Mark. *Pericles on 31st Street.* Chicago, Quadrangle Books, 1965. 213p.

ICU; IEN; IU; MnU; RPB; TxU; ViBlbV; WU PZ4.P4885Pe

Kazan, Elia. *The Arrangement.* New York, Stein and Day, 1966.

DLC; ICU; NjR; OCl; OCU; OO; CSt

Petrakis, Harry Mark. *Dream of Kings.* New York, McKay, 1966. 180p.

CtY; DLC; MeB; NN; OCl; ViBlbV PZ4.P4885Or

Mountzoures, H. L. *The Empire of Things and Other Stories.* New York: Charles Scribner's Sons, 1968.

DLC; CtY

PUBLICATIONS DEALING WITH THE GREEK ORTHODOX CHURCH IN THE UNITED STATES

Dournovo, N. N. "E Helliniki Ekklesia kai e Ethniki Anagennesis" [The Greek Church and National Regeneration], *Hellinismos,* III (January 1900), 200-212).
NN; OCU

Adeney, Walter F. *The Greek and Eastern Churches.* New York, Charles Scribner's and Sons, 1908.
DLC   BX290.A3

Orthodox Greek Wedding Ceremony. *Travel* (N.Y.), XIII (January 1908), 201-202.
CLU; DLC; PP; PSC; PLF (BIF)

Protestant Episcopal Church in the U.S.A. Province of New England Missionary Council. *A Report of the Commission Appointed . . . to Consider Cooperating with the Eastern Orthodox Churches, the Separated Churches of the East.* Springfield, Massachusetts, 1913. 120p.
The people of the Eastern Orthodox churches, the Separated Churches of the East, and other Slavs. Report of the commission appointed by the missionary department of New England to consider the work of cooperating with the Eastern Orthodox Churches, the Separated Churches of the East, and other Slavs. Presented at the Council of the Department held at Providence, Rhode Island, October 23, 1912.
CtY; NN

Lacey, Thomas J. *A Study of the Eastern Orthodox Church.* New York, 1912.
DLC; MnUIA; NN

Turkevich, Leonid. "Problems of the Eastern Orthodox Church in America," *Constructive Quarterly,* III (June 1915), 311-327.
At that time author rector of the Orthodox Ecclesiastical Seminary at Tenafly, New Jersey.
PLT

Galanos, Michael I. *The Church Issue of Greeks in America* [in Greek]. Chicago, 1924. 72p.
MH   Wid.-US10621.50

Joachim, K. K. *E Kindinoi tou en Ameriki Hellenismou kai ta Mesa tis Diasoseous Autou* [The Dangers Facing the Greeks of America and the Means for Their Salvation]. Boston, 1926.

MHCr; MHW   Wid.-US10621.55

Emhardt, William C. *Eastern Church in the Western World.* Milwaukee, 1928.

DLC; MnUIA; OCl; PPLT; PU

Polyzoides, Rev. Germanou. *Reader in Church History* [in Greek]. New York, D. C. Divry, Inc., n.d. [1933?]. 127p.

Reader in Greek Orthodox Church history which was to be used in the Greek Sunday schools in the United States ca. 1932.

DLC   BX290.P6CP2

Fernandez, W. G. Tinchon. "Eastern Orthodox Peoples and Churches in the United States," *Christendom*, IV (Summer 1939), 423-436.

CLSU; MH; NN; PLF

Athenagoras. "Will the Greeks in America Lose Their Racial Identity?," *Hellenic Spectator*, I, No. 5 (July 1940), 5.

Translation of remarks made by the then Bishop and Director of the Institute of Holy Cross, Columbia University, May 12, 1940.

NN

Rife, J. Merle. "Do Greeks Worship?," *Christian Century*, LVIII[2] (October 8, 1941), 1244-1245.

A letter to the editor describing the Greek Orthodox service in various cities of the United States. Author signed Muskingum College, New Concord, Ohio.

CSt; DLC; MH; NN; PLF

Papas, John. *The Greek Church in the Courts.* [Sanford, Maine, 1945?]. 132p.

MHCr   HC-Pi450PA

Papas, John. *The Scandals of the Greek Church.* [Sanford, Maine, 1945?]. 62p.

MHCr   HC-Pi450PA

Efthimiou, B. *Skiagrafia ton apodemon Hellenon tes Amerikes kai Historia tou Kathedrikou Neas Yorkes* [History of the Immigrant Greeks in the United States and History of the Cathedral of New York]. New York, Cosmos Greek American Printing Company, 1949. 207p. Bibliography, p. 11.

NN; MH   NYPL-IEE-Greek

Eastern Orthodox Church, North and South America. *The Historic Decision of the Tenth Biennial Ecclesiastical Congress at St. Louis.* New York, ca. 1950.
NN

Anonymous. *Twelfth Biennial Ecclesiastical Congress of the Greek Orthodox Church of North and South America.* Savannah, Georgia, 1954.
MHW

Upson, Stephen H. R. *Orthodox Church History.* Brooklyn, New York, Syrian Antiochian Orthodox Archdiocese of New York and All North America, 1954.
MHCr

Anderson, Paul B. "Eastern Orthodox Churches in the United States," *Information Service*, XXXIV, No. 43 (Saturday, December 24, 1955). 2 notes, including table.
PLF(BIF)

Hammond, Peter. *The Waters of Marah: Present State of the Greek Church.* London, Rockliff, 1956.
PP; PPLT; PPPD; PPT; PPWe

Athenagoras, Bishop. "Holy Cross Greek Orthodox Theological School: Twenty Years of Progress, 1937-1957," *The Greek Orthodox Theological Review*, III, No. 1 (Summer 1957), 15-22. Eight comments, bibliographical footnotes.
PLT; PLF(BIF)

Binsfield, Edmund L. "Church Archives in the United States and Canada: A Bibliography," *American Archivist*, XXI, No. 3 (July 1958), 311-332. 219 entries. Eastern Orthodox Church, p. 322.
CLU; DLC; MH; NN; NNC; PLF

Cavarnos, Constantine. *E Orthodoxia en Ameriki* [The Orthodox Faith in Amerika]. Athens, 1958.
MHCr

Dukakis, Constantine S. *Betrayal of a Sacred Trust.* August 18, 1958.
MB

44

Kourides, Peter T. *The Evolution of the Greek Orthodox Church in America and Its Present Problems.* New York, Cosmos Greek-American Printing Company, 1959. 62p.
MnUIA; NjPT

Dukakis, Constantine S. "The Proposed Hellenic University," *Philaletheia,* III (April 1961). 39 Russell Street, Arlington, Massachusetts. 9p.
MB; PLF(BIF)

Grigorieff, D. "Historical Background of Orthodoxy in America," *St. Vladimer's Seminary Quarterly,* V. No. 1-2 (1961), 3-53.
PLT

Anonymous. "The Orthodox Church in America: Past and Future," *St. Vladimer's Seminary Quarterly,* (1961).
PLT

Verkhovskoy, S. S. "Unity of the Orthodox Church in America," *St. Vladimer's Seminary Quarterly,* V, No. 1-2 (1961), 101-113.
PLT

Volaitis, Constantine. "Orthodox Church in the United States as Viewed from the Social Sciences," *St. Vladimer's Seminary Quarterly,* V, No. 1-2 (1961), 63-87. 34 notes includes bibliography.
NjP; PLF

Dukakis, Constantine S. *The Fate of the Greek Orthodox Church in America.* [Arlington, Massachusetts, 1962?].
MB

Dukakis, Constantine S. "The Fate of the Greek Orthodox Theological School," *Philaletheia,* II (January 1963), new edition. 18p.
PLF(BIF)

Wiest, Walter E. "The Centenary of the Greek Orthodox Archdiocese of North and South America," in A. J. Philippou (ed.), *The Orthodox Ethos, Studies in Orthodoxy.* Oxford, Holywell Press, 1964. Vol. 1, pp. 3-20.
PLF(BIF)

Gabriel, George. *Letter to Archbishop Iakovos for not Accepting Ordination, December 24, 1965.* 4p. (Mimeographed). Saint Nectarios Education Series, No. 9.
PLF(E-53)

Contos, Leonidas. *Guidelines for the Orthodox in Ecumenical Relations.* Published by the Standing Conference of Canonical Orthodox Bishops in America and commended to the clergy for guidance. 1966. 31p.

PLF(E-68)

Dukakis, Constantine S. "The Eastern Orthodox Church in Grave Danger," *Philaletheia,* IV (April 1966). 39 Russell Street, Arlington, Massachusetts. 32p.

PLF(BIF)

Constantelos, Demetrios J. *The Greek Orthodox Church: Faith, History, and Practice.* [Foreword by Archbishop Iakovos.] New York, Seabury, 1967.

DLC; PLF; PLT; PSt

Doumouras, A. "Greek Orthodox Communities in America Before World War I," *St. Vladimer's Seminary Quarterly,* II, No. 4 (1967), 172-192. 52 notes.

NjP

Tsoumas, G. J. "Founding Years of Holy Cross Greek Orthodox Theological School (1937-1942)," *Greek Orthodox Theological Review,* XII, No. 3 (1967), 241-282.

PLF(BIF); PLT

Dukakis, Constantine S. "Tragic Situation at the Greek Theological School," *Philaletheia,* V (April 1967). 39 Russell Street, Arlington, Massachusetts 02174. n.p. [8p.]

PLF(BIF)

Azkoul, Michael. "An Open Letter to the Orthodox Hierarchy," 1967? Also in *The Russian Orthodox Journal* (June 1968), 5p (Mimeographed). Saint Nectarios Education Series, No. 10.

PLF(E-53)

Holy Transfiguration Monastery. *Concerning Father Neketas Palassis and the Parish of St. Nectarios in Seattle, 1968.* 4p. (Mimeographed). Saint Nectarios Education Series, No. 5.

PLF(E-53)

Holy Transfiguration Monastery. *An Open Letter to the Logos, 1968.* 20p. Saint Nectarios Education Series, No. 1.

PLF(E-53)

Holy Transfiguration Monastery. *Second Open Letter of the Holy Transfiguration Monastery to the Logos, 1968.* 23p. Saint Nectarios Education Series, No. 3.
PLF(E-53)

Johnstone, John. *The Victory for Unity.* 1968. 5p. (Mimeographed). Saint Nectarios Education Series, No. 12.
PLF(E-53)

Palassis, Neketas, Rev. "The Greek Ecumenical Ideal," *Orthodox Christian Witness.* September 30 / October 13, 1968; October 7/20, 1968; October 14/27, 1968; October 28 / November 10, 1968. Saint Nectarios Education Series, No. 13.
PLF(E-53)

Catalog of Orthodox Icons, Religious Articles. January, 1969. [Seattle, Wash., 1969] [2]p. Eastern Orthodox religious items available from St. Innocent's Bookstore, Inc., 9223 - 20th Avenue, N. E.
PLF(E-53)

UNPUBLISHED WORKS

Lovejoy, Gordon William. "The Greeks of Tarpon Springs." Thesis (M.A.) — University of Florida, Gainesville, Florida, 1938. 182p. FU.

Antoniou, Mary. "Welfare Activities Among the Greek People in Los Angeles." Thesis (M.A.) — University of Southern California, 1939. 198p. figures; tables; map of Los Angeles "Greektown," p. 49; comprehensive bibliography, p. 172-194. CLSU.

Historical Records Survey, Inventory of the Church Archives in New York City. *Eastern Orthodox Churches.* [WPA, New York, 1940]. 178p. (Mimeographed) DLC; PLF [E-69: partial contents p. 113-124].

Keker, Joan. Miscellaneous Lore of Greeks in the United States, Michigan, Detroit, 1946. WFA No. 1946(22). 17p. [Xerox of original WSU student typed report owned by WFA-PLF (E-71)].

Mistaras, Evangeline. "A Study of First and Second Generation Greek Out-Marriages in Chicago." Thesis (M.A.)—University of Chicago, 1950. 114p. Bibliography, pp. 113-114. ICU.

Yerocaris, Constantine. "A Study of the Voluntary Association of the Greek Immigrants of Chicago from 1890 to 1948, with Special Emphasis on World War I and Post War Period." Thesis (M.A.)—University of Chicago, 1950. ICU.

Ethnic Groups in Detroit. Wayne State University, Department of Sociology and Anthropology. Detroit, 1951. Microfilm or photoprint available. Call No. 312.9 W 367e. MiDW.

Georgas, Demitra. "Greek Settlement of the San Francisco Bay Area." Thesis (M.A.) — University of California, Berkeley, June 1951. 84p. CU Micro No. 308t.G346.

George, Rose. Greek Folk Customs [Massachusetts and Michigan], 1951. WFA No. 1951(14). 36p. [Xerox of original WSU student typed report owned by WFA-PLF (E-71)].

Alatis, James E. "The Americanization of Greek Names." Thesis (M.A.)—Ohio State University, 1952. OU.

Halley, Hellen. "A Historical Functional Approach to the Study of the Community of Tarpon Springs." Thesis (Ph.D.)—Columbia University, 1952. 206p. Tables, bibliography on pages 201-206. DLC Micro.; NNC.

Markakis, John D. "The Influence of English Upon Modern Greek as Spoken in America." Thesis (M.A.)—Ohio State University, 1952. 137p. OU.

Jackson, Maria. "The American Greek Community in Bridgeport." Bridgeport, Connecticut, 1955. 22p. University of Bridgeport Community Area Study. Student monograph no. 7. Bibliography, p. 21. NN

Macris, James A. "An Analysis of English Loan Words in New York City Greek." Thesis (Ph.D.)—Columbia University (N. Y.), 1955. NNC

Michelis, Dennis. "In the Realm of Grace." [Warren, Ohio, 1956?] [60]p. (Mimeographed) illus. A series of lectures given by author as pastor of St. Demetrios Church, Warren, Ohio, in Winter, 1955-1956. PLF (E-74).

A Study of the Foreign Born Population of Detroit, 1870-1950. Wayne State University, Department of Sociology & Anthropology. Detroit, 1957. Original noncirculating, Microfilm; Photoprint Call no. 312.9 W 367 C. MiDW

Cutsumbis, M. N. "Greek-Americans—A Study of Anomie." [Columbus Ohio, 1957]. 36p. transcript (typewritten). PLF(BIF).

Theodoratus, Robert James. "The Influence of the Homeland on the Social Organization of a Greek Community in America." Thesis (Ph.D.)—University of Washington, 1961. 290p. Univ. Micro. order no. 61-6654.

Goshorn, John. "Conflict in a Greek Orthodox Parish: A Case Study." [Columbus, Ohio, 1962] 16p. transcript (typewritten). PLF(BIF).

Lagos, Mary. "A Greek Family in American Society." [Lima, Ohio, 1962] 8p. transcript (typewritten). PLF(BIF).

Koumaras, George S. The Founding of the Greek Orthodox Church and Community in Lancaster, Pennsylvania. June, 1963. [13]

p. [Xerox of original Millersville State College student typed report owned by Rev. Alexander Veronis, Lancaster — PLF (E-OV-4)].

Lefty, Sophia. Miscellaneous Lore of Greeks in United States [Michigan, Detroit], 1963. WFA No. 1963(76). 8p. [Xerox of original WSU student typed report owned by WFA-PLF(E-71)].

Doumouras, Alexander. "The Origins of the Greek Orthodox Church in America." 27p. B.D.D. Thesis, St. Vladimir's Orthodox Theological Seminary (Crestwood, N.Y.), 1964. [Xerox of original typed copy — PLF(BIF)].

Georges, Robert Augustus. "Greek-American Folk Beliefs and Narratives, Survival and Living Tradition." Thesis (Ph.D.)—Indiana University, 1964. 243p. InU.

Sigma Epsilon Phi Newsletter, April 1964. 8p. (Mimeographed). PLF(BIF).

Vlachos, Evangelos C. "The Assimilation of Greeks in the United States: with Special Reference to the Greek Community of Anderson, Indiana." Thesis (Ph.D)—Indiana University, 1964. 287p. Univ. Micro order No. 65-3528.

Buxbaum, Edwin C. "World View and Attitude in a Greek-American Ethnic Group." Thesis (M.A.)—University of Pennsylvania, 1965? 105p. PU

Molek, Mary. Bibliographic Data [Greek] in Immigrant Archives, May 27, 1965. [Minneapolis, Minnesota, 1967] 18p. (Xeroxed with note—"not for publication.") PLF(BIF)

Niforos, Lambro. The Evil Eye [Michigan, Detroit], 1965. WFA No. 1965(112). 22p. [Xeroxed of original WSU student typed report owned by WFA-PLF (E-71)].

Seaman, Paul David. "Modern Greek and American English in Contact: A Socio-Linguistic Investigation of Greek American Bilingualism in Chicago." Thesis (Ph.D.)—Indiana University, 1965. 451p. Univ. Micro. Order No. 65-10, 887.

Alatis, James E. "The American-English Pronunciation of Greek Immigrants: A Study in Language Contact with Pedagogical Implications." Thesis (Ph.D.)—Ohio State University, 1966. Univ. Micro. available.

Colovas, Anthone C. "The Icarian Community in the Detroit Area: Its Background and Its Marriage Patterns." Detroit, 1966. 28 p. [Xerox of original WSU student typed report owned by Detroit Public Library—Burton Collection—PLF(BIF)].

Fournaris, Theodore. "From Beaver Street to Suburbia." [Lancaster, Pa., 1966]. 16p. transcript (typewritten). PLF(BIF).

Markides, Kyriakos. "Assimilation of Greeks in Youngstown." Thesis (M.A.)—Bowling Green State University, Ohio, 1966? OBG.

Seder, Doris L. "The Influence of Cultural Identification on Family Behavior." Thesis (Ph.D.)—Brandeis University, 1966. 249p. Univ. Micro. Order No. 66-9451.

Buxbaum, Edwin Clarence. "The Greek-American Group of Tarpon Springs, Florida: A Study of Ethnic Identification and Acculturation." Thesis (Ph.D.)—University of Pennsylvania, 1967. 472p. Univ. Micro. Order No. 67-12, 733.

Kiriazis, James W. "A Study of Change in Two Rhodian Immigrant Communities." Thesis (Ph.D.)— University of Pittsburgh, 1967. Univ. Micro. Order No. 6807522.

Scourby, Alice. "Third Generation Greek Americans: A Study of Religious Attitudes." Thesis (Ph.D.)—New School for Social Research, 1967. 106p. Univ. Micro. Order No. 67-15, 926.

Bartholomew, Gilbert L. Annunciation Orthodox Church (Lancaster, Pa.): Organizational Structure and Administration, May 1, 1968. 5p. [Xerox of original PLT student typed report owned by Rev. Alexander Veronis, Lancaster—PLF(E-OV-4)].

Clubb, Jerome M. Progress Report on Historical Data Projects, May 10, 1968 (Revised). Inter-University Consortium for Political Research, Ann Arbor, Michigan. 19p. (Mimeographed). PLF(E-73).

Frey, Sara A. "The Greeks in Memphis (Tennessee): An Early History." [Memphis, Tenn., 1968?] 16p. (Mimeographed) footnotes p. 14-16. PLF(E-10).

Fournaris, Theodore J. "A Study of the Opinions of Greek-Americans of Lancaster County on the Question of Church Involvement in Civil Rights." January 20, 1968. [Lancaster, Pa. 1968] 12p. transcript (typewritten) PLF(BIF).

Institute of Texan Cultures. Greek Histo-Wall Complete. Items pertaining to Greeks in Texas. Appeared in the Greek Exhibit Section of Texas Pavilion at Hemisfair, 1968. [San Antonio, Texas, 1968] [25]p. (Mimeographed) 41 items annotated. PLF (BIF).

Lammers, Thomas. Membership of Hellenic Orthodox Church of the Annunciation (Lancaster, Pennsylvania), 1968. 8p. [Xerox of original PLT student typed report owned by Rev. Alexander Veronis, Lancaster—PLF(E-OV-4)].

Peeler, David G. History of "Annunciation" Hellenic Orthodox Church (Lancaster, Pa.). April 1, 1968. 9p. [Xerox of original PLT student report owned by Rev. Alexander Veronis, Lancaster—PLF(E-OV-4)].

Veronis, Alexander. Report of the Foreign Missions Program of the Greek Orthodox Archdiocese of North and South America. Paper presented during the 19th Clergy-Laity Congress, Athens, Greece, July 20-27, 1968. 7p. [Xerox of mimeographed copy owned by author—PLF(E-OV-4)].

Wanjau, G. E. Program, Annunciation Greek Orthodox Church, 64 Hershey Avenue., Lancaster, Pennsylvania, November 30, 1968. 7p. [Xerox of original PLT student typed report owned by Rev. Alexander Veronis, Lancaster—PLF(E-OV-4)].

Patler, John. Biographical Materials Obtained from The Northern Virginia Sun Newspaper and by personal interview, April 3, 1969, at Arlington, Virginia. PLF(E-82).

ALMANACS, GUIDES AND DIRECTORIES

Xanthaky, Socrates Anthony. "The Greeks' Companion." New York, The "Atlantis," 1903. 282p. fold map.
A general guide for Greeks in the United States and Canada. Greek and English text. Advertising matter included, p. 275-282.
DLC; MB; NN; PU   E184.G7X2

Hēmerologion Thermopylōn Kai Hellēnikos Hodēgos Tēs Amerikēs (Almanac and Greek Guide of America). New York, Thermopylae Publishers, 1904. 404p.
Greek and English text. Advertising matter included.
DLC; NN   E184.G7H4

Canoutas, Seraphim George (comp.). Hellēnikos Emporikos Hodēgos (Greek-American Guide and Business Directory). New York, Greek Commercial and Bureau, Inc., 1907. illus., ports. [First edition].
English and Greek text. Advertising matter included.
DLC; NN   E184.G7H4

Canoutas, Seraphim George ((comp.). Directory of the Greek Business Men in the United States & Canada. New York, Phoenix Printers, 1909. 404p.
English and Greek text. Advertising matter included.
NN   NYPL-IEE-Greek

Canoutas, Seraphim George. Greek Immigrant's Guide. New York, Helmis Press, 1909. 124p. illus., ports. M. A. Sabbaidēs, joint author.
English and Greek text. Advertising matter included.
DLC; NN   JV6545.G7C3

Canoutas, Seraphim George (comp.). Greek-American Guide and Business Directory. New York, Helmis Press, 1912. 503p.
English and Greek text. Advertising matter included.
NN   NYPL-IEE-Greek

Helmis, George N. *Greek-American Guide and Business Directory*. New York, Helmis Press, 1915. 342p.

English and Greek text. Advertising matter included.

NN   NYPL-IEE-Greek

Canoutas, Seraphim George. *O Symboulos kai Proheiros Dikegoros tou Hellinos en Ameriki* (The Adviser and Handy Lawyer of the Greek in America). New York, Cosmos Press, 1917. 333p.

English and Greek text. Advertising matter included.

DLC; MH; NN   JV6545.G7C4

Gkines, Michael. *American Cookery for Non-English Speaking Cooks*. New York, The "Atlantis," 1917. 320p.

Includes menus with suggested prices. Greek text. Advertising matter included.

ICJ (Levis Collection)

Prometheus Publishing Company. *The Greeks in California, Their History and Achievements, 1918-1919*. San Francisco, 1919.

CU-B; WaU

Tsākonas, Aristotle Spyridon. *Learning the United States through printed work in the Principal Foreign Languages*. Philadelphia, 1920. 11p.

English and Greek text.

DLC   LC3731.T7

Greek Directory of Chicago and Vicinity. Chicago, Nicholson Brothers, 1921. illus.

DLC; NN   F548.9.G7G7

Canoutas, Seraphim George (ed.). *United States and Canada Greek Business Directory*. New York, Greek Commercial and Information Bureau, Inc., 1921.

English and Greek text.

DLC; NN   NYPL-IEE-Greek

Papamanoli, Hercules N. *Perilyptiki Historia tou Kanada kai Hellino-Kanadikos Odigos* (Comprehensive History of Canada and Greek-Canadian Guide). Montreal, 1921-1922.

NN   NYPL-IEE-Greek

Nickolson, Nick, George Nickolson, Sam Nickolson. *Greek Directory of 1923*; covering Illinois, Indiana, Iowa, Michigan, Minnesota, Wisconsin. Chicago, Greek Directory Publishing Company, 1923. 480p. illus., ports.

Advertising matter included.

DLC; MiD; NN   E184.G7G7

Associated Greek Press of America. *Greek Business Guide and Directory of the Western States.* San Francisco, 1925.

NN   NYPL-IEE-Greek

The Greek Blue Book; a Purchasing Guide for 50,000 Greek-American Business Establishments. New York, Greek Blue Book, Inc., 1939. 91p.

NN   NYPL-TLE

Polenēs, Em. *Enkolpion Metanastou* (The Immigrants Manual). Athens, 1945. 138p. ports.

DLC   G469.P6

Hellenic-Americans of Los Angeles and Vicinity. Directory. [Hollywood, 1946] 85p. illus., ports.

DLC   F869.L8H4

Desfis, Angelos. *Hellenic Americans of Arizona and Los Angeles and Vicinity.* Directory. Hollywood, 1947. 85p. illus., ports.

DLC; NN   F820.G7H4

GREEK-AMERICAN SERIALS CURRENTLY PUBLISHED

Ahepan. v. 1+ 1923+ Washington, D.C. 6 times a year.
  Title varies: 1 & 2 as the order's *Bulletin*; v. 3-13 no. 5, My
  1929- Ag. 1939 *Ahepa.* English text. DLC 3+; MdBe 5+; NN
  3+; 00 10+

Athenai (Detroit Athens). 1928+. Weekly. Greek text. MiD

The Athene. v. 1+ November 1940+ Chicago. Quarterly. English
  text. DLC 1+; IC 1+; MH 1+

Atlantis. 1894+ New York. Daily and Sunday. Greek text.
  NN [Mar. 2, 1895 - Dec. 10, 1897; Jan., 1906 - July 31, 1913;
  Jan., 1919 - Dec. 31, 1922; June - Aug., 1939].

Atlantis. [1894+?] New York. Monthly, illus. Greek text. NN

Challenge. v. 1+ February, 1963 - Spring 1967+? [Washington,
  D.C.]. Frequency varies. English text.
  A publication of St. Sophia Greek Orthodox Cathedral, Wash-
  ington, D.C. PLF (E-62-63).

The Chicago PNYX. 1941+. Semi-monthly. English text. cf. *Yearbook,* 1966-1969.

Concern. [1968+?] New York. Quarterly. English text. cf. *Yearbook,* 1968-1969.

Crete (Kriti). 1927+ New York. Monthly. Greek text. cf. *Yearbook,* 1966-1969.

Cyprus Official publication of the Cyprian Federation. New York.
  Greek text. cf. *Yearbook,* 1966-1969.

Elleniki Zoi (Southern Hellenic Life). San Francisco. Bimonthly.
  Greek text. cf. *Yearbook,* 1966-1969.

Ellenikos-Aster (Greek Star). 1904+ Chicago. Weekly. English
  text. Title varies: *Aster,* Mar. 18, 1904 - Jan. 3, 1908.
  Suspended N 1950 - Ag. 30, 1951
  IC Jan., 1904 - Jan., 1908; Micro. IC Jan., 1908 - April, 1910;
  IU 1909+; WHi 1915+

Ethnikos Kyrix (National Herald). April 2, 1915+ New York. Daily and Sunday. English and Greek text. ICRL April 2, 1915 - Dec. 31, 1923; NN

Goyan (Greek Orthodox Youth of America). v. 1+ 1953+ Chicago. Bimonthly. English text. DLC [1]+ MH-AH [6, 8]

G.O.Y.A. Bulletin. New York. Bimonthly. English text. cf. *Yearbook,* 1966-1969.

Greek Orthodox Theological Review. v. 1+ August, 1964+ Brookline, Massachusetts. Biannually. English text. CtY-D 1+; ICU 1+; MBu-T 1+; NNUT 1+; NjPT 1+; PLT 1+; TxDaM 1+; CtHT 1+; IU 1+; MoSC 1+; NcD 1+; OU 1+.

Greek Press. 1912+ Chicago. Weekly. Greek text. Micro. IC June 1929 - Mar. 1934; Micro DLC July 16, 1942-45.

Hellenic Free Press. 1957+ Chicago. Semimonthly. Greek text. cf. *Yearbook,* 1966-1969.

Hellenic Chronicle. Boston. Weekly. English text. cf. *Yearbook,* 1966-1969.

Hellenic News. 1963+ New York. Monthly. Greek text. cf. *Yearbook,* 1966-1969.

Hellenic Review & International Report. 1959+ New York. Monthly. English text. Title varies: N 1959 - Oc. 1960, *Hellenic Review & Economics, Trade, Shipping, Travel.* AMAU [1]+; CU [1]+; CLU [4]+; MH 1+; NN 1+; MiEM 2+.

Kypiakatika Nea (The Greek Sunday News). 1950+ Boston. Weekly. English and Greek text. cf. *Yearbook,* 1966-1969.

National Greek Tribune. 1920+ Detroit. Weekly. Greek text. cf. *Yearbook,* 1966-1969. MiD.

The New California. 1907+ San Francisco. Weekly. Greek text. cf. *Yearbook,* 1966-1969.

New York. 1948+. Monthly. Greek text. cf. *Yearbook,* 1966-1969.

O Logos. St. Louis, Missouri. 6 times a year. English text. cf. *Yearbook,* 1966, 1968-1969.

The Logos. v. 1+ 1968+ Fort Wayne, Indiana. [Monthly]. English text. PLF (E-72).

Macedonia. New York. Monthly. Official Publication of Macedonian Federation. Greek text. cf. *Yearbook,* 1966-1969.

The Orthodox Observer. v. 1+ 1934+ New York. Monthly. English and Greek text. NNG 1+; DS 22+.

O Fanos. 1961+ New York. Monthly. Greek text. cf. *Yearbook,* 1969.

Roumeli Press. 1965+ New York Monthly. Greek text. cf. *Yearbook,* 1967-1969.

The Tribune of GAPA. v. 1+ 1936+ Pittsburgh, Pennsylvania. 5 times a year. Greek text. IU [5]+.

Greek-American Serials Suspended with Holdings and References Provided

American Greek. v. 1-2 January 1920 - January 1921. New York. Monthly. English and Greek text.
"Official organ of Greek-American Merchants Protective Association of America." NN; cf. NYPL.

American Greek Review. v. 1-6 June 1923 - January 1928 Chicago. Monthly. Title varied: June 1923 - December 1924, *Greek Review,* v. I-II. CU [1-]+; CtY 1+; DLC 1+; MH 1+; MnU 1+; NN 1+; OCl 1-2; OrCA [2+]; OrU 1+; PP 1+ cf. WPA-COP, p. 61; ULS, 3rd.

American Hellenic World. v. I-V March 17, 1924? - December 19, 1931? Chicago. Monthly. Numbering irregular.
Published as weekly from 1924-1927; as monthly from 1927-1930. cf. Saloutos, (1964) p. 399 gives March 28, 1925 - December 19, 1931. CSt [4-5]; DLC 2+; NN [1]+; Micro IC Aug. 1926 - Oct. 1928. cf. WPA-COP, p. 61.

Archon Magazine. v. 1-2 July - August 1927 Philadelphia. illus., ports. Monthly. "Devoted to the interests of the fraternal order of the Ahepa." NN cf. NYPL, cat.

Argonautes. v. 1-2 1959-1962 New York. illus., ports. English and Greek text. MH; NN. cf. Widener and NYPL cats.

Athena. 1905-1913 Chicago. Semi-weekly. ICHi Sep. 17, 1906. cf WPA-COP, p. 62; IA, p. 3.

California. 1908?-1920? San Francisco, California. Weekly. CU. cf. NOM; IA, p. 3.

Chicago Greek Daily. 1921-1935 Chicago. Micro IC 1921-32, 1934-Jan. 1935. cf. COP, p. 8.

Democrat. 1927-1931 Chicago. NN 1927 - April 1931; Micro IC 1927-1931. cf. Saloutos, 1964, p. 398; COP, p. 8.

Democratis (Democrat). 1924-1930 Chicago. Monthly. Greek text. NN, 1924-1929. cf. WPA-COP, p. 62; IA, p. 4.

Eastern and Western Review. v. II?-IX 1909?-1916 Boston. MB; MH. cf. Saloutos, 1964, p. 399; IA, p. 4.

Eleutheros Typos (Free Press). 1944-1946 New York. Personal possession of Theodore Saloutos, Los Angeles, California. cf. Saloutos, 1964, p 398.

Empros (Forward). January 1925-1927 New York. NN. cf. Saloutos, 1964, p. 398.

Greek News. 1935 st? & exp? Chicago. Weekly. Micro IC, 1935, cf. COP, p. 8.

Greek News. Los Angeles. Weekly. DLC. cf. IA, p. 8.

Greek-American News. Mar. 15, 1936+? Chicago. Semi-monthly. Micro IC, 1936. cf. COP, p. 8.

Greek-American. v. I-II December 1927 - May 1928 New York. NN; DLC. cf. Saloutos, 1964, p. 399; IA, p. 6.

Greek American Council Bulletin. v. 1-4 October 7, 1944-1947 New York. Frequency varied.
Title varied: *The Greek American Committee for National Unity,* Oct. 7, 1944 - Feb. 1945; *American Council for a Democratic Greek,* Oct. 1946 - Feb. 1947. MB. cf. BPL cat.

Greek-American Review. v. I-II March 1917 - April 1918 Boston. MB; NN [I-II]. cf. BPL cat.; Saloutos, 1964, p. 399.

Hellenic Renaissance. v. 1-2 May 1919 - July 1919 Chicago. Monthly. DLC. cf. WPA-COP, p. 64.

Hellenic Spectator. v. I February 1940 - February 1941 Washington, D.C. illus. No issue for April 1940. NN. cf. NYPL cat.; Saloutos, 1964, p. 399.

Loxias (The Blade). June 17, 1908 - April 25, 1919 Chicago. Weekly. Micro IC, June 1908 - Nov. 1918; IU, Aug. 29, 1917 - Apr. 25, 1919. cf. COP, p. 8; WPA-COP, p. 65.

National Union. v. 1-2 April 1928 - November 1930 Springfield, Mass. Frequency varied. illus., ports.
"An educational progressive magazine for the advancement of new Americans... Springfield, Mass.: The American Hellenic Union, Inc., 1928-30?. Subtitle and numbering varied. cf NYPL cat.; Saloutos, 1964, p. 399.

PanHellenic Union. v. 1-2 February 15, 1914 - December 19, 1915 New York. NN; MH. cf. NYPL cat.; ULS 3rd.

Philhellene. v. I-IX January 1, 1942 - 1950 New York. Frequency varied.
"Bulletin of the American Friends of Greece" subtitle. cf. v. 1, no. 1. MH (Culolias, Notebook H-VIII, Storage 57, Box no. 1of 5. Incomplete holdings: v. II, III, IV, V-VI, VII-VIII are missing)

Proodos (Progress). April 1931?-1937 Chicago. Frequency varied. Published in Detroit, Mich., 1918-1931. Micro IC Apr. 1931-Oct. 1934. cf. COP, p. 8; WPA-COP, p. 65; IA, p. 15.

Protoporos (Pioneer). v. I-III March, 1935 - June 1937 New York. Monthly. "Organ of... Greek Workers' Educational Federation of America." cf. NYPL cat.; Saloutos, 1964, p. 399.

Saloniki-Greek Press. 1912?-1936 Chicago. Weekly. Superceded *Thessaloniki* when *Thessaloniki* merged with *Greek Press,* Mar. 29, 1934. Micro IC, Aug. 1913-1931 (as *Saloniki*); Micro IC, Mar. 1934-1936 (as *Saloniki Greek Press*); IC, 1917 - Feb. 8, 1919 as *Thessaloniki*); IU, 1917 - Jan. 1, Apr. 1921-34 (as *Thessaloniki*); cf. COP, p. 8; WPA-COP, p. 66.

The Vineyard. v. 1+ 1968+ New York. Monthly? English text. Published by the Brotherhood of Saint Mark of Ephesus. 535 84th Street, Brooklyn, N. Y. 11209. Editor: Deacon Photios Touloumes. Editorial Board: George Gabriel, Antony Gavelas. PLF(E-80) has Vol. 1, No. 2, 1968; Vol. 11, No. 1, 1969.

Campana. v. 1+ 1917+ New York, N.Y. Semi-monthly. Greek text. Publisher & Editor: Costas Athanasiades, 360 W. 36th Street, New York 10018. "Independent Greek-American Review." IA. cf. IA, p. 11.

FRATERNAL PUBLICATIONS

The AHEPA. Annual Convention, Order of AHEPA [American Hellenic Educational Progressive Association], Washington, D.C., No. 6 [Washington, D.C., 1928].
NN   NYPL-SKV

The AHEPA. Official Program National Convention, Order of AHEPA, No. 11 [Columbus, Ohio?, 1934?]. illus., ports.
NN   NYPL-SKV

Chryssikos, George John. The Heritage of Lacedaemonians and the American Opportunities. New York, 1938. Reprinted from the 1936 Yearbook of the Association of Lacedaemonians.
NN   NYPL-IAG p.v. 769

Demeter, George C. *AHEPA Manual.* Official Guide of the Order of AHEPA containing early history and miscellaneous fundamentals of the Order adopted by the Fourth Annual Convocation. Boston, Athens Printing Company, 1926. 210p. illus.
MH   Wid.-Soc 9001.5

Greek-American Progressive Association. Fourth Annual Convention, Detroit, Michigan, 1929. n.p. illus., ports.
Advertising matter included. MiD. J. Burton Collection. No. E&M 74.D4 325.2495.

Greek Orthodox Community, Huntsville, Alabama. Directories of Membership [n.d.]. Inquiries invited: Rev. Iakovos Kotrokois.

Greek Orthodox Youth of America. Sixth Annual Districts 1-2, Diocese V, G.O.Y.A. Conference, June 15-17, 1962. Charleston, South Carolina [Charleston, S.C., 1962] [20]p. ports.
Brochure includes: "Aims" and "principles" of the Greek Orthodox Youth of America, p. [17]; "Why a Junior G.O.Y.A.?," p. [18]; Statements made to Conference by Archbishop Iakovos, Rev. Nicholas C. Trivelas and Bishop Germanos Polyzoides, p. [1,3,4]. Advertising matter included. See also, p. 69, entry "Assumption. . . Denver, Colorado. Program Album. . ."

a message sent to clergy-laity Congress (Colo. 1964) by Patriarch Athenagoras I, Istanbul, June 4, 1964, p. [9].

PLF (E-68)

Greek Orthodox Youth of America. Six District Conference, Diocese IX, District 1, Watertown, New York, June 2-4, 1967. [Watertown, N.Y., 1967] [44]p. illus., ports.

Brochure includes a statement made to Conference by Archbishop Iakovos, New York, May 3, 1967, p. [2]. Advertising matter included.

PLF (E-68)

Greek Republican Club, Boston, Massachusetts. Greek Republican Members of Massachusetts, 1920. 2p. transcript (typewritten). Folder 7/10, Greek Community in Boston. Box 12x9¾x4¼". N. Culolias papers.

MH

Hellenic Association of Boston. Souvenir Program, Twelfth Annual Ball. Boston, Massachusetts: Friday, May 2, 1919, Paul Revere Hall.

MH (US 10621 10), also notebook H-IX Nicholas Culolias papers.

Hellenic Association of Boston. Katastatikon. 1920-1922. Contains names of officers and members.

MB   BPL-*3078.248

Hellenic Association of Boston. Annual Ball, 13th. Souvenir Program. . . April 21, 1920.

MB   BPL-44509.168

Kalymnos Society. Annual Charity Entertainment and Ball. New York, 1936. illus. English and Greek text.

NN   NYPL-SIA

Pan Hellenic Union. Katastatikon tēs (by-laws of) Pan Hellenic Union. New York, The Helmis Press, 1914. 31p.

NN   NYPL-HAE p.v. 628

Pan Hellenic Union. Katastatikon tēs (by-laws of) Pan Hellenic Union, Boston. New York, Cosmos, 1910. 64p. Greek and English text.

NN   NYPL-HAE p.v. 88

Pan Rhodian Society, Warren, Ohio. Twenty-fifth Annual Convention of the Pan-Rhodian Society "Apollon" of America, July 4th - 6th, 1952, Warren, Ohio. [Warren, Ohio, 1952] [108]p. illus., ports.

Includes: Notices from other chapters, *passim*. Advertising matter included.

PFL (E-78)

Panchiaki, Koraes, Society, New York. Tenth Annual Convention of the United Chios Societies of America, August 31st - September 4th, 1950, New York. [New York, 1950] 88p. ilus., ports.

Includes: Notices from other chapters, *passim*; lists names of officers. Advertising matter included.

PFL (E-77)

Panchiaki, Koraes, Society, Philadelphia, Pennsylvania. Twelfth Annual Convention of the United Chios Societies of America, July 2-5th, 1953, Philadelphia, Pennsylvania. [Philadelphia, Pa., 1953] [86]p. illus., ports.

Includes: Notices from other chapters, *passim*; names of officers. Advertising matter included.

PFL (E-77)

Pyrrhus Benevolent Society, Inc. Twenty-fifth Anniversary Pyrrhus Benevolent Society, Sunday, January 19, 1941, Manhattan Center, New York. [New York, 1941] 144p. illus., ports. Greek text.

NN   NYPL-SIA

United Chios Societies of America, Steubenville, Ohio. 13th Annual Convention of the United Chios Societies of America, July 1-4th, 1955, Steubenville, Ohio. [Steubenville, Ohio, 1955] [66]p. illus., ports. Advertising matter included.

PLF (E-77)

United Chios Society of America, Warren, Ohio. 17th Bi-ennial National Convention, June 27-30, 1963, Warren, Ohio. [Warren, Ohio, 1963] [84]p. illus., ports.

Includes: Program; list of names of officers; notices from other chapters, *passim*. Advertising matter included.

PLF (E-77)

PARISH AND ARCHDIOCESAN MATERIALS

All Saints Greek Orthodox Church, Peoria, Illinois. *Dedication Book, June 20, 1965.* [Peoria, Ill., 1965] [68]p. ports.

"As We Saw It. . ." a brief history of the Greek Community in Peoria from 1902-1965, p. [14-17]. Advertising matter included.

PLF (E-1)

St. Andrew Greek Orthodox Church, South Bend, Indiana. Yearbooks and Directories since date established, 1927?

Available in Church Library Archives.

Inquiries invited: Rev. George C. Massouras

Annunciation Greek Orthodox Church, Baltimore, Maryland. *Fiftieth Anniversary Souvenir Book. . .1906-1956.* [Baltimore, Md., 1956] 158p. ports.

Names of past parish presidents, p. 16. A brief history of the community, p. 19-25. Members of congregation, p. 51-63. Advertising matter included.

PLF (E-2)

Annunciation Hellenic Orthodox Church, Columbus, Ohio. 1959 Members ond Non-Members (partial list). 1958 Members (partial list). [19]p.

Transcripts (typewritten) from addressograph paper tape [Columbus, Ohio, 1959].

PLF (E-3)

Annunciation Greek Orthodox Church, Dayton, Ohio. Membership Directory, 1967. [Dayton, Ohio, 1967] 29p. (Mimeographed)

PLF (E-4)

Annunciation Greek Orthodox Cathedral, Detroit, Michigan. *Golden Anniversary Album, 1961.* [Detroit, Mich., 1961] [66]p. illus., ports.

A brief history of community, p. [10-11]. Advertising matter included.

PLF (E-5)

Annunciation Greek Orthodox Church, Dover, New Hampshire. *Consecration Album,* 1966. [Dover, N.H., 1966] [154]p. illus., ports.

A brief history of the community, p. [20-26]. Advertising matter included.

PLF (E-6)

——. Membership List (1968?). [Dover, N.H., 1968] 9p. (Mimeographed). Address included.

PLF (E-6)

Annunciation, Church of the, Elkins Park, Philadelphia, Pennsylvania. Afternoon Greek Language School Commencement Exercises, June 16, 1968, Program. [Elkins Park, Philadelphia, Pa., 1968] [10]p.

Pamphlet lists: Honor Graduates of the Afternoon School, p. [6]; Sunday School Pupils, 1967-1968, p. [7-8]; Faculty, p.[10].

PLF (E-7)

——. New Building Project Appeal. [Elkins Park, Philadelphia, Pa., 1968] [16]p.

Brochure lists: New building committee members, and Annunciation parish and council, 1968, p. [1] fold.

PLF (E-7)

——. The 147th Anniversary of the Greek Independence Day and 67th Name Day Celebration of the Church of the Annunciation, Saturday, March 30, 1968. [Elkins Park, Philadelphia, Pa., 1968] [84]p.

Brochure lists: Parish Council (1966), p. [11]; Patrons, Contributors and members of the parish, p. [79-84]. Includes advertising matter.

PLF (E-7)

Annunciation, Church of, Elkins Park, Philadelphia, Pennsylvania. Directory of Membership, 1966.

Inquiries invited: Rev. Paul G. Economides

Annunciation Greek Orthodox Church, Kansas City, Missouri. Church Directory, 1968, Third Edition. [Kansas City, Mo., 1968] 40p.

"The Community," p. 5-11. "Members of the Church Community," p. 12-35. Advertising matter included.

PLF (E-8)

Annunciation, Hellenic Orthodox Church of the, Lancaster, Pennsylvania. 1960 Membership Directory. [Lancaster, Pa., 1960] 8p. (Xeroxed)

Includes names of officers of various parish committees and organizations.

PLF (E-9)

——. May 1962 Membership Directory. [Lancaster, Pa., 1962] 19p. (Xeroxed)

Includes names of officers of various parish committees and organizations.

PLF (E-9)

——. 1967 Membership Directory. [Lancaster, Pa., 1967] 23p. (Mimeographed)

Includes names of officers of various parish committees and organizations.

PLF (E-9)

——. Annual Congregational Meeting of Sunday, December 11, 1966, 2:00 P.M. [Lancaster, Pa., 1966] 14p. (Mimeographed)

PLF (E-9)

——. Annual Congregational Meeting, December 15, 1968. [Lancaster, Pa., 1968] 17p. (Mimeographed)

PLF (E-9)

——. Building Fund Report, December 15, 1968. [Lancaster, Pa., 1968] 13p. (Mimeographed)

PLF (E-9)

——. Parish Newsletters and Memorandums, September, 1967 - October, 1968. [Lancaster, Pa., 1967+]

PLF (E-9)

Annunciation Hellenic Orthodox Church, Memphis, Tennessee. *Dedication Book, Sunday, August 28, 1955.* [Memphis, Tenn., 1955] 112p. illus., ports.

"The History of the Greek Orthodox Church in Memphis," p. 20-23. Advertising matter included.

PLF (E-10)

——. 1968 Mailing List of the Annunciation Greek Orthodox Community. [Memphis, Tenn., 1968] 6p. (Mimeographed)

PLF (E-10)

Annunciation Greek Orthodox Church, Milwaukee, Wisconsin. 1967 Members' Contribution List. [Milwaukee, Wis., 1967] 38p.
PLF (E-11)

——. Miscellaneous Materials dealing with the Annunciation Greek Orthodox Church of Milwaukee designed by Frank Lloyd Wright in 1958.
PLF (E-11)

Annunciation Greek Orthodox Church, Newburry, Massachusetts. Greek Orthodox Community Annunciation Membership Directory, February 1, 1965. [Newburyport, Mass., 1965] [6]p. (Mimeographed)
PLF (E-12)

Annunciation Greek Orthodox Church, Norfolk, Virginia. *50th Anniversary Dedication Album, 1961.* [Norfolk, Va., 1961] [124]p. illus., ports.
"Fifty Years of Progress," p. [12-18]; "The Priest Who Served Our Community," p. [10]; "The Presidents of Our Community," p. [11]. Advertising matter included.
PLF (E-13)

——. Parish Membership Directory. 1968? [Norfolk, Va., 1968?] 18p. (Mimeographed)
PLF (E-13)

St. Anthony Greek Orthodox Church, Springfield, Illinois. Partial Membership List. One page typescript (original copy) with stamped signature of Rev. Fr. Basil Apostolos [Springfield, Ill., 1968].
PLF (E-14)

Archangel Michael Greek Orthodox Church, Campbell, Ohio. *Dedication Album, November 11, 1956.* [Campbell (Youngstown), Ohio, 1956] [96]p. Illus., ports.
"This Is Our Story..." a brief history of the parish from 1919-1956, p. [15-16]. Advertising matter included.
PLF (E-15)

——. Tenth Anniversary, 1955-1965, November 13-14, 1965. [Campbell (Youngstown), Ohio, 1965] [88]p.
"Congregation of Archangel Michael Greek Orthodox Church," p. [85-88]. Advertising matter included.
PLF (E-15)

Ascension, Greek Orthodox, Church of, Oakland, California. Hellenic Community of Oakland and Vicinity. [Oakland? Calif., 1961?] 1 v. (unpaged) illus., ports.

CU-B

Assumption Greek Orthodox Church, Erie, Pennsylvania. Community Life, KOIMISIS TIS THEOTOKOY, GREEK ORTHODOX CHURCH. BULLETIN. [Erie, Pa.]

Was to be published bi-monthly with Volume I (unspecified), February, 1966 [13]p. (Mimeographed); Volume II, May, 1966 [18]p. (Mimeographed) advertising matter included p. [18]; Volume III, November, 1967, [7]p. (Mimeographed)

PLF (E-16)

Assumption Greek Orthodox Church, Denver, Colorado. *Program Album, Seventeenth Biennial Ecclesiastical Clergy-Laity Congress and Philoptohos Conference of the Greek Archdiocese of North and South America, Centennial Observance Year, June 28 - July 4, 1964.* Hosted by The Greek Orthodox Church "Assumption" of the Hellenic Orthodox Community of Denver, Colorado. [Denver, Colo., 1964] [364]p. illus., ports.

"History of the Greek Archdiocese of North and South America, (1922-1964)," p. [57-58]; "History" of the Greek Orthodox Community of Denver, p. [126-127]. Advertising matter included.

PLF (E-17)

Assumption Greek Orthodox Church, Port Jefferson, New York. *Annual Grecian Ball of the Greek Orthodox Church of the Assumption, Port Jefferson, New York, Sat., Dec. 2, 1967.* Middle Island Country Club. [Port Jefferson, N.Y., 1967] [60] p. illus., ports.

"Recipes," p. [43-46]; "Glossary and Translations of Food Ingredients," p. [47]; "Parishioners," p. [48-60]. Advertising matter included.

PLF (E-18)

Assumption Greek Orthodox Church, Poughkeepsie, New York. "A Short History of Our Church." [Poughkeepsie, N.Y., 1967] [2]p. Xeroxed copy.

PLF (E-19)

St. Athanasius Greek Orthodox Church, Arlington, Massachusetts. *Parish Information Brochure.* [Arlington, Mass., 1968?] [6]p. illus., ports.

PLF (E-20)

St. Barbara Greek Orthodox Church, Durham, North Carolina. Membership Directory, February, 1967. [Durham, N.C., 1967] [9]p. illus., ports. Advertising matter included.

PLF (E-21)

St. Constantine Greek Orthodox Church, Chicago, Illinois. *Year Book of St. Constantine Church and Koraes School, 1936.* [Chicago, 1937]

IC (Listed under title)

SS. Constantine and Helen Greek Orthodox Church, Orange, New Jersey. *Cornerstone Book of the New Church Building.* [Orange, N.J., 1967?]

Historical Book Jubilee, 1917-1967. [Orange, N.J., 1967]

Parish Directory of Membership, 1967. [Orange, N.J., 1967]

Inquiries invited: Rev. George Mamangakis

SS. Constantine and Helen Greek Orthodox Church, Reading, Pennsylvania. Building Appeal Brochure, 1968. [Reading, Pa., 1968] [17]p. illus., ports.

PLF (E-22)

———. Parish Directory for 1967. [Reading, Pa., 1967] 10p. (Mimeographed).

PLF (E-22)

———. Patriarchate Ball, Sunday, November 27, 1955. [Reading, Pa., 1955] 48p. ports.

Brochure lists parish committees, p. 6-8. Advertising matter included.

PLF (E-22)

Sts. Constantine and Helen Greek Orthodox Church, Richmond, Virginia. Addresses and Home Phone Numbers of the Members of Sts. Constantine and Helen Greek Orthodox Church. [Richmond, Va., 1968?] 15p. (Mimeographed).

PLF (E-23)

Sts. Constantine and Helen Greek Orthodox Church, Webster, Massachusetts. *Fortieth Anniversary Souvenir Album, Sun-*

day, November 21, 1965. [Webster, Mass., 1965] [30]p. illus., ports.

Brochure lists: Charter members of the church, p. [1]; Priests who served the church from 1919-1965, p. [3]. "A Brief History of Our Church," from 1919-1965, p. [4-6]. "A Brief History of Philoptochos Society—25th Anniversary" from ca. 1924-1962, p. [9-10]. Advertising matter included.

PLF (E-24)

———. *Thyranoixia Album, May 26, 1968.* [Webster, Mass., 1968] [40]p. ports.

Brochure lists: "Church Council," 1968-1969, p. [13]; "Building Committee," p. [13]. Advertising matter included.

PLF (E-24)

———. Thyranoixia Program, Sunday, May 26, 1968. [4]p. illus., ports.

Leaflet lists: "Thyranoixia Committees," p. [3]; "Church Councils" from 1967-1969, p. [4]; "Building Committee," p. [4].

PLF (E-24)

St. Demetrios Greek Orthodox Church, Daytona Beach, Florida. *Twelfth Anniversary, 1964. Building Toward the Future.* [Daytona Beach, Fla., 1964] [56]p. illus., ports.

Commemorative brochure includes: "History of St. Demetrios Church," from 1952-1960, p. [6-7]; "Membership Directory," a list of all members and non-members compiled in November of 1963, p. [20-21]. Advertising matter included.

PLF(E-25)

St. Demetrios Greek Orthodox Church, Fall River, Massachusetts. Members and Contributors List, 1967-1968. [Fall River, Mass., 1968] [2]p. Transcript (typewritten) with printed attachment.

PLF (E-26)

St. Demetrios Greek Orthodox Church. Seattle, Washington. *Dedication Book, March 31, 1963.* [Seattle, Wash., 1963] [112]p. illus., ports.

A listing of: "past presidents" 1917-1962, p. [20]; "St. Demetrios Parish Priests, Since the Parish's Founding," p. [20]; "Building Committee Members Since 1942," p. [21]; "History of St. Demetrios Church," by Dorothy Mootafes—brief history

of Seattle's Greek Orthodox Community from 1895-1962, p. [22-25]. Advertising matter included.
PLF (E-27)

St. Demetrios Greek Orthodox Church, Upper Darby, Philadelphia, Pennsylvania. St. Demetrios Dinner Dance, Saturday, October 29, 1966, Sheraton Hotel, Philadelphia, Pennsylvania. [Upper Darby, Philadelphia, Pa., 1966] [60]p. illus., port.
Brochure listing: "Community Board of Trustees," "St. Demetrios" and "Annunciation" "Boards of Trustees," p. [60]. Advertising matter included.
PLF (E-28)

———. Third Annual Harvest Ball of The Greek Orthodox Community of Philadelphia, Annunciation, St. Demetrios, 1965. [Upper Darby, Philadelphia, Pa.] [682]p. illus.
Brochure listing: "Community Board of Trustees," "St. Demetrios" and "Annunciation" "Board of Trustees," p. [68]. Advertising matter included.
PLF (E-28)

St. Demetrios Greek Orthodox Church, Warren, Ohio. Thirty-fifth Annual Dance of the Hellenic Orthodox Church Saint Demetrios, Sunday, Oct. 25, 1953, Armory Hall, High Street, Warren, Ohio. [Warren, Ohio, 1953] [36]p. illus., ports.
Brochure lists: Officers and members of Parish Council, 1953, p. [5]. Advertising matter included.
PLF (E-29)

———. Hellenic Orthodox Church, First General Assembly (Annual), Sunday, January 29, 1961, Agenda. [Warren, Ohio, 1961] [1]p. (Mimeographed).
PLF (E-29)

———. List of Donors for Sunday, Holiday & Name Day Envelopes for 1960. [Warren, Ohio, 1961] [13]p. (Mimeographed).
Included Financial Statement for 1960-1961, p. [11-13].
PLF (E-29)

———. *Greek Orthodox Church St. Demetrios, Dedication Album, November 13th, 1960, Warren, Ohio.* [Warren, Ohio, 1960] [178]p. illus., ports.
A listing of: Past presidents and priests (in Greek), p. [27]. "A Brief History of the St. Demetrios Greek Orthodox Church

of Warren, Ohio," ca. 1917-1958, p. [25-26]. English and Greek text. Advertising matter included.

PLF (E-29)

St. Demetrios Greek Orthodox Church, Warren, Ohio. *Saint Demetrios Hellenic Educational and Community Center.* [Warren, Ohio, 1967?] [20]p. illus.

Appeal Brochure includes: "A Brief on Our Community's Past...," ca. 1917-1960s, p. [17]. Members of the fund raising drive, p. [20]. Descriptions of proposed center.

PLF (E-29)

Dormition of the Virgin Mary Greek Orthodox Church, Sommerville, Massachusetts. Yearbook & Directory of Membership, 1968?.

Inquiries invited: The Very Reverend Christodulous Kallos.

St. Elias the Prophet. Dedication and Directory of Membership, 1957, Dubuque, Iowa. Annual Membership List.

Inquiries invited: Rev. Evangelos N. Kasemeotes

St. George Greek Orthodox Church, Asbury Park, New Jersey. *Consecration-Dedication Album, April 27 & 28, 1963.* [Asbury Park, N.J., 1963] 64 p. ports.

Brochure includes: "St. George Greek Orthodox Community Its History and Growth," from ca. 1926-1963, p. 46-54. Lists "Past Presidents, Deceased," "Past Presidents, Living," and "Board of Directors," p. 21-23.

PLF (E-30)

———. Greek Orthodox Community, Annual Year Book, 1967-68. [Asbury Park, N.J., 1968] 48p. ports.

Brochure includes: "Board of Directors," p. 1. Advertising matter included.

PLF (E-30)

St. George Greek Orthodox Church, Des Moines, Iowa. "Saint George" Greek Orthodox Community, Des Moines, Iowa, Church Bulletin, 1965, Tenth Edition. [Des Moines, Iowa, 1965] 31p.

Brochure includes: Presidents and clergymen of community from 1928-1965, p. 11-13. "Members of Church and Community Des Moines," p. 21-30. Advertising matter included.

PLF (E-31)

St. George Greek Orthodox Church, Hyannis, Massachusetts. Membership List, 1968. [Hyannis, Mass.] [5]p. (Mimeographed).
PLF (E-32)

St. George Greek Orthodox Church, Knoxville, Tennessee. 4th Annual Edition of "Greek Nite" Program Book and Community Directory, October, 1968. [Knoxville, Tenn., 1968] 92p. illus., ports. "Benefit [Brochure] of the St. George...Building Fund." Advertising matter included.
PLF (E-75)

St. George Greek Orthodox Church, New Bedford, Massachusetts. *50th Aninversary, 1910-1960 Book.* [New Bedford, Mass., 1960] [56]p. ports.
Brochure includes: "The History of the Saint George Greek Orthodox Church," by Reverend Constantine Bebis from ca. 1910-1958, p. [16-18]. Advertising matter included.
PLF (E-33)

St. George Greek Orthodox Church, New Britain, Connecticut. *Golden 50th Anniversary Album, 1915-1965.* [New Britain, Conn., 1965] [112]p. illus., ports.
"Presidents of the Parish," 1916-1962, p. [10-11]; "Pastors of the Parish," 1916-1954, p. [12-13]; "First Parish Board of 1916 and Charter Members," p. [15]; Members' names of parish during 1916, p. [16-17]; "History of the Community of St. George," ca. 1915-1964, p. [18-23]. English and Greek text. Advertising matter included.
PLF (E-34)

St. George Greek Orthodox Church, Pontiac, Michigan. Twentieth Anniversary of the St. George Greek Orthodox Community of Pontiac, Michigan, 1928-1948. [Pontiac, Mich., 1948] 40p. (Xeroxed copy).
Brochure includes: "Historical Note," ca. 1920-1935, p. 3; "1928" and "1948" "Board of Directors," p. 5; Presidents & pastors from 1928-1948, p. 17; "Business Establishments of Members," p. 19-21; "1948 Active Membership," p. 23-33. Advertising matter included.
PLF (E-35)

St. George Greek Orthodox Church, Shreveport, Louisiana. The "St. George" Greek Orthodox Community, Church Directory, 1968. [Shreveport, La., 1968] [20]p.

Brochure lists: Priests of the community from 1916-1963, p. [4]. "A Brief History of the Greek Orthodox Community of Shreveport, Louisiana," ca. 1912-1957, p. [7-9].
PLF (E-36)

St. George Greek Orthodox Church, Springfield, Massachusetts. List of Names of "Head of Families," 1967. [Springfield, Mass., 1967] [3]p. Xeroxed with 2"x 5 ¼" clipping stapled on third page. Irregular size of pages.
Material obtained from Rev. Stephen Papadoulias, 1968.
PLF (E-37)

St. George Tropaioforos, New York, New York. Yearbooks and Directories of Membership. Publications since date of founding (?).
Inquiries invited: Rev. Soterios Metrakos.

Holy Cross Greek Orthodox Church, Belmont, California. Greek Orthodox Church of the Holy Cross, 1964-1965, Album-Directory. [Belmont, Calif., 1965] [54]p. ports.
Brochure includes: "Historical Review," ca. 1956-1964, p. [2-9]; 1964, 1965 Parish Councils, p. [12]; "Members of Greek Orthodox Church of the Holy Cross, Alphabetical Listing of Names, Addresses and Telephone Numbers," p. [21-36]. Advertising matter included.
PLF (E-38)

——. Directory, Summer, 1968. Belmont, Calif., Holy Cross Press, 1968. 24p. ports.
Brochure lists officers for various parish organizations, p. [i].
PLF (E-38)

——. Greek Orthodox Church of the Holy Cross, Belmont, California. Belmont, Calif., Holy Cross Press, 1968. 6p.
Pamphlet on design & iconography of the Greek Orthodox Church.
PLF (E-38)

Holy Cross Greek Orthodox Church, Pittsburgh, Pennsylvania. 1965-1966 Directory. [Pittsburgh, Pa., 1966] 36p. illus.
Brochure includes: "Historical Milestone of Holy Cross Church," ca. 1950-1965, p. 21-23; Parish committees and or-

ganization membership, p. 23-28; Financial statement from 1954-1964, p. 30. Advertising matter included.

PLF (E-39)

——. 1967-1968 Directory. [Pittsburgh, Pa. 1968] 34p. ports.

Brochure includes: "Historical Milestones of Holy Cross Church, 1950-1967," p. 24-26; Parish committees and organizations membership, p. 26-29; Financial statement from 1954-1966, p. 31. Advertising matter included.

PLF (E-39)

Holy Mother of God Greek Orthodox Church, Tallahasee, Florida. [Directory, as of July 5, 1968] [Tallahasee, Fla., 1968] [7]p. ports.

Pamphlet includes: "A Short History of the Tallahasee Parish," ca. 1941-1965, p. [2]; "Baptized & Chrismated Membership as of July 5, 1968," p. [5-7]. Advertising matter included.

PLF (E-40)

Holy Transfiguration Monastery. Letter to John Johnstone, Jr., Kirkwood, Missouri, on the Calendar Issue. n.d. [1968?] 8p. (Mimeographed). Saint Nectarios Education Series, No. 2.

PLF (E-53)

Holy Trinity Greek Orthodox Church, Charleston, South Carolina. *Progress Souvenir Book, Greek Community, Cornerstone Laying Ceremonies, March 4-5, 1951, Charleston, South Carolina.* [Charleston, S.C., 1951] 92p. ports.

"A History of the Greek Community of Charleston, S.C.," from 1911-1951, p. 46-47. "Veterans of World War II," p. 51. Also names of officers of certain parish organizations, *passim*. Advertising matter included.

PLF (E-41)

——. *May 17, 1953, Dedication Book.* [Charleston, S.C., 1953] [86] p. ports.

A brief historical description of all fraternal organizations connected with the Greek community of Charleston, p. [37-41]. Advertising matter included.

PLF (E-41)

——. Golden Anniversary Banquet, Francis Marion Hotel, Sunday, December 4, 1960. [Charleston, S.C., 1960] [4]p.

Leaflet includes: Program on p. [3].

PLF (E-42)

———. *Fiftieth Anniversary, 1910-1960, December 3 and 4, 1960.* [Charleston, S.C., 1960] [64]p. illus., ports.

A brief history of the parish and Greek community, 1910-1960, p. [3, 13, 19, 25, 29]. "Officers of Board of Directors, 1910-1960," p. [43, 45]. Advertising matter included.

PLF (E-42)

———. *Church Directory, August, 1968 Edition.* [Charleston, S.C., 1968] 21p.

PLF (E-42)

Holy Trinity Greek Orthodox Church, Chicago, Illinois. *Forty Years of Greek Life in Chicago, 1897-1937.* Chicago: Aristotle Damianou, Printer, October 16, 1937. [239]p. illus., ports.

Memorial Album includes: Statements to the Parish from Patriarch Benjamin I (Istanbul, Aug. 1937), Archbishop Chrisostomos of Athens (Athens, August 7, 1937), p. [, 6]; Holy Trinity Parish Councils, 1897, 1937, p. [8]; "Hull House," p. [54-61]. Contains much material concerning the Chicago Greek Community, *passim*. Greek text. Advertising matter included.

PLF (E-43)

Holy Trinity Greek Orthodox Church, Concord, New Hampshire. Twenty-seven years of Progress of the Greek Orthodox Community..., 1930-1957. [Concord, N.H., 1957] 110p. illus., ports. Greeks in New Hampshire. New Hampshire State Library, Concord.

Holy Trinity Greek Orthodox Church, Fond Du Lac, Wisconsin. Golden Anniversary Album, September 29, 1968.

Inquiries invited: Rev. Nicholas Liberis.

Holy Trinity Greek Orthodox Church, Holyoke, Massachusetts. Information on Composition of Parish.

Inquiries invited: Rev. Harry Vulopas.

Holy Trinity Greek Orthodox Church, Lewiston, Maine. 1917-1967 Souvenir Program, Golden Anniversary Celebration, April 15 and 16, 1967. [Lewiston, Me., 1967] [8]p. ports.

Pamphlet includes: "Greek History" a brief history of the Greek community in Lewiston-Auborn area from ca. 1900-1965, p. [3]; Officers of Parish Council and program committee members, p. [6].

PLF (E-44)

Holy Trinity Greek Orthodox Church, Lewiston, Maine. *Anniversary Album, 1917-1967.* [Lewiston, Me., 1967] [122]p. illus., ports.

"Our Local History" a brief history of Lewiston Greek Community from ca. 1900-1967, p. [22-23]. Includes lists of priests and presidents of community and bishops visiting the church, 1910-1967, p. [24]; Family names of parishioners, p. [51]. English and Greek text. Advertising matter included.

PLF (E-44)

Holy Trinity Greek Orthodox Church, Orlando, Florida. Fifth Anniversary, October, 1968. [Orlando, Fla., 1968] [52]p. illus., ports.

Brochure includes: A brief history of Orlando Greek Community, ca. 1926-1963, p. [15,17,18]; "The Challenge," p. [20]. Advertising matter included.

PLF (E-45)

Holy Trinity Greek Orthodox Church, Steubenville, Ohio. Holy Trinity Herald, 1967. [Steubenville, Ohio, 1967] [44]p. illus., ports.

Brochure lists: "1967 Board of Directors," p. [9]; Community organizations officers, p. [1]. English and Greek text. Advertising matter included.

PLF (E-46)

Holy Trinity Greek Orthodox Church, Westfield, New Jersey. Third Annual Dance, Friday, September 27, 1968. [Westfield, N.J., 1968] [80]p. illus., port.

Brochure listing: Parish Council Members, p. [2]. Advertising matter included.

PLF (E-47)

Holy Trinity and St. John the Divine, Jackson, Mississippi. Directory of Membership [n.d.].

Inquiries invited: Rev. John G. Kallimanis

Holy Trinity Greek Orthodox Church, Wilmington, Delaware. Harvest Dance, November 18, 1962. [Wilmington, Del., 1962] [48]p. ports.

Program Brochure lists: Officers and members of the Board of Trustees, p. [2]; program officers, p. [25]. Advertising matter included.

PLF (E-48)

St. John the Baptist Greek Orthodox Church, Anaheim, California. The Greek Orthodox Church of Orange County... Annual Benefit Dinner Dance, Saturday, November 26, 1966. [Anaheim, Calif., 1966] [32]p. illus., ports.

Brochure lists: "1966 Board of Directors," p. [8-9]; "Past presidents," 1961-1965, p. [11]; Church Membership Directory, p. [30-32]. Advertising matter included.

PLF (E-49)

——. Directory of 1967 Members and New Members Pledging for 1968. [Anaheim, Calif., 1967] 4p. (Mimeographed).

PLF (E-49)

St. John Greek Orthodox Church, Youngstown, Ohio. *Golden Anniversary, 1915-1965, Sunday, November 7, 1965.* [Youngstown, Ohio, 1965] [16]p. illus., ports.

Brochure includes: "Anniversary Committee," p. [9]; "An Historical Synopsis," ca. 1915-1950, p. [10]; "Board Members," 1915-1964, p. [11-13]; "Parish Priests," p. [14]. English and Greek text. Advertising matter included.

PLF (E-50)

St. Katherine Greek Orthodox Church, Falls Church, Virginia. St. Katherine Greek Orthodox Church of Northern Virginia, Falls Church, Virginia, 1964. [Falls Church, Va., 1964] [144]p. illus., ports.

Commemorative Album includes: Brief "History of St. Katherine...," p. [10-19]; "Membership Directory," p. [138-143]. Advertising matter included.

PLF (E-51)

——. Saint Katherine's Greek Orthodox Church of Northern Virginia, Sixth Annual Dance, Friday, October 15, 1965. [Falls Church, Pa., 1965] [92]p. ports.

Brochure includes: "Parish Directory," p. [6]. Advertising matter included.

PLF (E-51)

——. Souvenir Album, 1967. [Falls Church, Va., 1967] 40p illus., ports.

Brochure includes: "Parish Directory," p. 10.

PLF (E-51)

St. Katherine Greek Orthodox Church, Redondo, California. Church Directory, (1970?).

Inquiries invited: Rev. Fred Fotion

Kimissis Thetokou, Racine, Wisconsin. Parish Yearbook (n.d.).

Inquiries invited: Rev. Peter N. Pappademetriou

St. Luke Greek Orthodox Church, Broomall, Pennsylvania. The Third Annual Show and Dance of the St. Luke. . . Community of Delaware and Montgomery Counties of Pennsylvania, Benefit—Building Fund, Saturday, September 14, 1963, Sheraton Hotel-Philadelphia. [Broomall, Philadelphia, Pa., 1963] [64] p. illus.

Brochure lists: "Executive Officers," "Board of Trustees," p. [5]; "Committees," p. [9-10]. Advertising matter included.

PLF (E-52)

——. Membership Directory. [Broomall, Philadelphia, Pa., 1968?] [11]p. stapled (Mimeographed).

Brochure lists: "Parish Council Officers," p. [1]; "Council Members," p. [2].

PLF (E-52)

——. "A Brief Biographical Sketch of St. Luke." [Broomall, Philadelphia, Pa., n.d.] 1p. (Mimeographed).

PLF (E-52)

St. Mary's Greek Orthodox Church, Minneapolis, Minnesota. Yearbooks and Directories available on site.

Inquiries invited: Rev. Anthony Coniaris

St. Nectarios American Orthodox Church, 9223 20th Avenue, N.E., Seattle, Washington 98115. One of the parishes of Greek Orthodox Americans who have attempted to dissociate from the Greek Orthodox Archdiocese and to affiliate with the Russian Orthodox Church Outside Russia. Reverend Neketas Palassis has issued a series of pamphlets and leaflets outlining the conservative position he and his parish of St. Nectarios have adopted since 1968. Although Metropolitan Filaret of the Russian. . . Russia is not a participant of the Standing Conference of Canonical Orthodox Bishops in the Americas, the Greek Orthodox Church is in full communion with that church. (See: Greek Orthodox Archdiocese of North and South America, 1967 *Yearbook*, p. 69; *Ibid.*, 1968 *Yearbook*, p. 155; in 1969

Yearbook, p. 120, the Russian Orthodox Church Outside Russia was not included as one of the churches in communion with the Greek Orthodox Archdiocese.)

PLF (E-53)

St. Nicholas Greek Orthodox Church, Baltimore, Maryland. Yearbooks and Directories of Membership. Publications since date of founding, 1955(?).

Inquiries invited: Rev. Peter C. Chrisafideis

St. Nicholas Greek Orthodox Church, Bethlehem, Pennsylvania. Parish Directory for Bethlehem, Allentown and Vicinity, 1968? [Bethlehem, Pa., 1968] 14p. (Mimeographed)

PLF (E-54)

St. Nicholas Greek Orthodox Church, Lexington, Massachusetts. Membership Directory, 1968. [Lexington, Mass., 1968] [9]p. (Mimeographed)

Pamphlet includes: "Officer & Board Members," p. [1-2]; "Parish Membership," p. [3-7]; "Financial Statements—1967," p. [8-9].

PLF (E-55)

St. Nicholas Greek Orthodox Cathedral, Pittsburgh, Pennsylvania. *Consecration Album, The Greek Community of Allegheny... Pittsburgh, Pennsylvania, May 13, 1962.* [Pittsburgh, Pa., 1962] 64p. ports.

Brochure includes: Chronology of parish events, ca. 1904-1962, p. 12-46; Membership of Cathedral, p. 56-59; "The Greek Community of Allegheny County," p. 60-61; Founders of parish, (port.) p. 62. English and Greek text. Advertising matter included.

PLF (E-56)

———. Greek Community of Allegheny County, *60th Anniversary Album, 1906-1966.* [Pittsburgh, Pa., 1966] 140p. illus., ports. Brochure lists: "Parish Council," p. 13; "Clergy and Layleaders... 1906-1966," p. 14; "Founding Fathers (port.)," p. 15. English and Greek text. Advertising matter included.

PLF (E-56)

St. Nicholas Greek Orthodox Church, Wilmington, North Carolina. Church Directory, 1967-68. [Wilmington, N.C., 1968] [12]p. Brochure with advertising matter included.

PLF (E-57)

St. Paul Greek Orthodox Church, Parma Heights, Ohio. Membership Directory, 1968?

Inquiries invited: The Reverend Theo. Anastasakis

St. Paul Greek Orthodox Church, Savannah, Georgia. *Sixtieth Anniversary. . . 1907-1967.* [Savannah, Ga., 1967] 72p. ports.

Brochure includes: Brief history by decades, p. 8, 14, 18, 28, 34, 44. Advertising matter included.

PLF (E-58)

————. Community Telephone Directory. 60th Anniversary Edition including Brunswick, Ga., Beaufort, S.C. Savannah, Ga. [Savannah, Ga., 1967] [28]p.

Brochure includes: "Recipes" for Prosphoron (offering loaf), "Kolyva" (Memorial Services boiled wheat), p. [22-25]. "Fasting in the Greek Orthodox Church," p. [26-28]. Advertising matter included.

PLF (E-58)

Savior, Church of Our, Rye, New York. 1967 Membership List. [Rye, N.Y., 1967] [6]p. (Mimeographed). Pamphlet.

PLF (E-59)

St. Sophia Greek Orthodox Cathedral, Los Angeles, California. Yearbook since date established, available on site.

Inquiries invited: Rev. Theophilos P. Theophilos

St. Sophia Greek Orthodox Cathedral, Washington, D.C. *Sixtieth Anniversary Commemorative Album . . . November 19, 1965.* [Washington, D.C., 1965] [162]p. ports.

A list of past officers and clergy, 1904-1965, p. [30-31]. Advertising matter included.

PLF (E-60)

————. *Commemorative Album . . . October 20, 1967.* [Washington, D.C., 1967] [148]p. ports.

A list of past officers and clergy, 1904-1967, p. [2]. Advertising matter included.

PLF (E-61)

————. *Saint Sophia Cathedral, Challenge.* February, 1963 - Spring, 1967. A publication of St. Sophia Cathedral. No numbering, irregular dating. English and Greek text.

PLF (E-62-63)

St. Sophia Greek Orthodox Church, New London, Connecticut. *Consecration... Album, November 7, 1965.* [New London, Conn., 1968] [24]p. illus., ports.

Brochure includes: "History" of parish, p. [3-4]; Consecration Program, p. [14-16]; "Past Presidents and Priests of the Parish," original building fund, p. [17]; Parish organizations, p. [19]; Donors of church furnishings, p. ([20-23]; Benefactors, Donors, and Patrons, and Friends, p. [23-24].

PLF⁺ (E-76)

——. Mailing List, November, 1968. [New London, Conn., 1968]. 12p. (Mimeographed).

PLF (E-76)

——. "Present Parish Council St. Sophia Church and Council Members. [1968-69?]" [New London, Conn., 1968?] 1p. 3"x10"

PLF (E-76)

St. Spyridon Greek Orthodox Church, Newport, Rhode Island. *Fiftieth Anniversary, 1915-1965.* [Newport, R.I., 1965] [56]p. illus., ports.

Brochure includes: "History of the Church," p. [16-28]. English and Greek text. Advertising matter included.

PLF (E-64)

——. Forty-Fifth Anniversary Ball... 1915-1960. [Newport, R.I., 1960] 72p. ports.

Brochure lists: "Board of Trustees," p. 9; "Executive Committee," p. 7; "History of Greek Community," p. 13-15. Advertising matter included.

PLF (E-64)

——. Forty-Seventh Anniversary Ball... 1915-1962. [Newport, R.I., 1962] 48p. ports.

Brochure lists: "1962 Board of Trustees," p. 9; "Executive Committee," p. 7. Advertising matter included.

PLF (E-64)

——. Forty-Eighth Anniversary Ball... 1915-1963. [Newport, R.I., 1963] 56p. ports.

Brochure lists: "1963 Board of Trustees," p. 9; "Executive Committee," p. 7. Advertising matter included.

PLF (E-64)

————. 1915-1965 ... Fiftieth Anniversary Banquet, Sunday, September 19, 1965. [Newport, R.I., 1965] [6]p.

Pamphlet lists: "Past Presidents," p. [5]; "Parish Council, 1965," p. [6].

PLF (E-64)

Taxiarchae Greek Orthodox Church, Watertown, Massachusetts. *Fifth Anniversary... Souvenir Book, 1956.* [Watertown, Mass., 1956] 57p. ports.

Brochure includes: Brief history of community 1923-1956, p. 14-15. English and Greek text. Advertising matter included.

PLF (E-65)

Taxiarchae Greek Orthodox Church, Watertown, Massachusetts. Annual Dinner Dance, Saturday, October 19, 1968. [Watertown, Mass., 1968] [20]p.

Brochure includes: "History of ... 1923-1968," p. [3-4]. Advertising mater included.

PLF (E-65)

Transfiguration of Our Savior, Lowell, Massachusetts. *Consecration, 1924-1964 ... October 18, 1964.* [Lowell, Mass., 1965?] [158]p. illus., ports.

Brochure includes: "Brief history of Our Parish," p. [17]; "Priests of Our Church [with ports.]," p. [18-19]; "past parish presidents," p. [20]; "past presidents of AHEPA, Lowell Chapter", p. [91]; Professional directory, p. [143-146]; "patrons," p. [147-152]. English and Greek text. Advertising matter included.

PLF (E-79)

St. Vasilios Greek Orthodox Church, Peabody, Massachusetts. Yearbooks and Directories since date of establishment, available on site.

Inquiries invited: The Reverend Neophytos Spyros

Zoodochos Peghee Greek Orthodox Church, Hot Springs, Arkansas. "History of the 'Zoodochos Peghee' Greek Orthodox Church." [Hot Springs, Ark., 1968?] 2p. transcript (typewritten).

Lists first church officers and board of trustees, p. 1.

PLF (E-66)

————. Membership List, 1968 [Hot Springs, Ark.] 5p. (Mimeographed).

PLF (E-66)

☆

Greek Orthodox Archdiocese of North and South America. St. Basil's Academy, Garrison, New York, Catalogue [New York, N.Y., 1968?] [47]p. illus., ports.

Catalog Brochure includes: Calendar, p. [1]; Board of Trustees and Administration, p. [3]; Faculty, p. [4-5]; General information related to the school, p. [6-20]; Curriculum, p. [21-32]; List of graduates from 1948-1967, p. [33-36]; 1968 class, p. [37].
PLF (E-68)

————. ————. Home for Children, Garrison, New York. [Garrison, N.Y., 1968?] [10]p. illus., ports., information pamphlet.
PLF (E-68)

————. Department of Education. Course of Study Prescribed for the Greek-American Elementary Schools. A Six Year Basic Program for Greek-American Education. Prepared by: Philippus D. Emmanuel. Brooklyn, New York: Kianis Press, Inc., [1958?] 90p.

Brochure includes: Names of "Educational Council," [1958?], p. iii; Introduction [in English], p. ix-xii; "The Six-Year School Graduate," p. 81-82 [in English]. Greek text.
PLF (E-67)

————. ————. Greek Education in America, School Year, 1965-1966. [New York, N.Y., 1966] [24]p. (Mimeographed).

A report dealing with Greek-American, Day and Afternoon Schools for 1965-1966. A list of the suggested readers. Summary of educational statistics are provided for each state. Includes names of Professors and Instructors of Greek descent teaching in the United States, [1966?]. Greek text.
PLF (E-67)

————. ————. Greek-American Parochial Schools. [New York, N.Y., n.d. [1967?] [1]p. (Mimeographed).

Lists names of school, address, and names of principals.
PLF (E-67)

————. ————. Greek American Day Schools. [New York, N.Y., n.d. (1967?)] [1]p. Xerox copy.

Gives statistics for Day and Afternoon schools, Kindergartens and Night schools.
PLF (E-67)

——. ——. A List of Approved Educational Books. [New York, N.Y., n.d. (1967?] [1]p. (Mimeographed).

Approved alphabet books and readers used from First Grade to Eighth Grade, Kindergarten and Afternoon schools. Greek text.

PLF (E-67)

——. ——. "Verified List" Ancient Greek in High Schools, Colleges and Universities [U.S.A.]. [New York, N.Y., n.d. (1967?)]. 3p. (Mimeographed).

Includes Modern Greek in High Schools, Colleges and Universities, p. 3.

PLF (E-67)

——. Department of Laity. New York, n.d. [1966?] 15p. diagr., illus., ports., tables.

Information brochure: "What is the Archdiocese," "How does the Archdiocese function?," p. 4; Departments of the Archdiocese, p. 5-7; "What are the Archdiocese institutions?," p. 8-10; "the ecumenical movement," p. 11; "Archdiocese special projects," p. 12; "How is the Archdiocese financed," p. 13; "the Archdiocese and your parish and you," p. 14. A summary note (in Greek), p. 2.

PLF (E-67)

——. Department of Press and Information. News Releases, March 31, 1967 - December 16, 1968. (Mimeographed) Incomplete.

Beginning with "The Holy Cross Greek Orthodox Theological School..." and ending with, "Christmas Message by Archbishop Iakovos to be read in Greek Orthodox Churches on December 22, New York, New York, December 16, 1968."

PLF (E-67)

——. Hellenic College. *Hellenic College, School of Arts and Sciences, 1968-1969.* [Brookline, Mass., 1968] [63]p. illus., ports.

Catalog brochure includes: Calendar, 1968-69, p. [2]; Board of Trustees and President's Council, p. [3-5]; College Council, Administration and Faculty, p. [6-13]; General information, p. [14-28]; Courses of instruction, p. [29-61].

PLF (E-68)

——. ——. *Hellenic College, Holy Cross School of Theology, 1968-1970.* [Brookline, Mass., 1968] [57]p. illus., ports.

Catalog brochure includes: Calendar, 1968-69, p. [2]; Board of

Trustees and President's Council, p. [3-5]; College Council, Administration and Faculty, p. [6-11]; General information, p. [12-28]; Courses of instruction, p. [29-42]; Student body, 1968-1969, Alumni, 1942-1968, p. [43-53].
PLF (E-68)

———. Holy Cross Orthodox Theological School. "Chronicle of the Holy Cross Orthodox Theological School," in *Greek Orthodox Theological Review*: Volume II, No. 1, 1956, p. 125-127; Volume II, No. 2, 1956, p. 105-111; Volume III, No. 1, 1957, p. 110-119; Volume III, No. 2, 1957, p. 238-243; Volume IV, No. 1, 1958, p. 195-199.
Lists names of faculty of the Holy Cross School for that year. Also the names of the incoming and matriculating students and graduates for that year.
PLT

———. ———. Catalog Issue, 1962-1963, Bulletin No. 6, October, 1962. 73p. Alumni of school from 1942-1962; Students in course, 1963; faculty, 1962, courses given.
MH, N. C. Culolias notebook H-IX

———. Office of Publication. The Lifting of the Anathema of 1054 as a Step Toward Reconciliation. [New York, N.Y., 1966] 39p. At head of title: "... Be Reconciled to Your Brother" (Matthew 5:24), p. 1, "The Nullification of the Anathema Between the Churches and Its Effect on the Relation Between the Greek Orthodox and Roman Catholic Churches." English and Greek text.
PLF (E-67)

———. ———. *1966 Desk Calendar and Yearbook*. [Bethlehem, Pa. 1966] 104p. (Lithographed) illus., ports, tables.
For most of the parishes listed [p. 66-92] the following information is also provided: Year parish organized; membership no. (1964); vital statistics, i.e., no. baptisms, marriages, funerals (1964); no. Sunday Schools (1964); Greek Schools (1964); church organizations (1964); assets and liabilities (1964); parish income and receipts (1963); Forwarded to Archdiocese (1964). Financial Statement for 1964, p. 65. Includes names of the faculty and officers for each Archdiocesan Institution, p. 57-64. English and Greek text. Advertising matter included.
PLF (E-69)

————. ————. *1967 Yearbook*. [New York, N.Y., 1967] 192p. illus., ports.

"Financial Statements for 1965," p. 108-111 are missing. Vital Statistics of the Archdiocese, p. 133. Includes names of the faculty and the officers for each Archdiocesan institution, p. 84-103. English and Greek text. Advertising matter included.
PLF (E-69)

————. ————. *1968 Yearbook* [New York, N.Y., 1968] 240p. illus., ports.

Includes: "Statement of Revenues and Expenditures for the Year Ended December 31, 1966 and 1965," p. 118; Resume of 1967 Approved Budget," p. 119; Names of the faculty and the officers for each Archdiocesan institution, p. 123-143. English and Greek text. Advertising matter included.
PLF (E-69)

————. ————. *1969 Yearbook* [New York, N.Y., 1969] 222p. illus., ports.

Includes: A brief glossary of Greek Orthodox terms, p. 70-75; directory of sustaining members, p. 208-215; names of the faculty and the officers for each Archdiocesan Institution, p. 122-150. English and Greek text. Advertising matter included.
PLF (E-69)

MANUSCRIPT COLLECTIONS

Annunciation Hellenic Orthodox Church, Lancaster, Pennsylvania. Parish Meetings Minutes, 1921-1954, [complete] (Xerox copies of handwritten transcripts).
PLF (E-OV-1-2)
Parish Meetings Minutes, 1955-1966, [partial] (Xerox copies of handwritten transcripts).
PLF (E-OV-2-3)
Baptismal, Death, Wedding Registers, 1932-1966 [complete] (Xerox copies of handwritten transcripts).
PLF (E-OV-4)
Miscellaneous materials, 1921-1968. (Xerox copies).
PLF (E-OV-4)

Billings, Lucille (Formerly Loukrata Gerasimos). Theodore M. Gerasimos Scrapbook. 1915-1964. 2v. John Burton Collection, Detroit Public Library.

Chian Brotherhood, St. Markella, Warren, Ohio. Minutes from 1933-1968. 2v. transcripts (handwritten). Greek text.
Inquiries invited: Michael N. Kondoleon, Warren, Ohio.

Culolias, Nicholas. Papers and Manuscripts on Greeks in Boston and Elsewhere. ca. 5 ft. In Houghton Library, Harvard University.

St. Demetrios Greek Orthodox Church, Warren, Ohio. Parish Meetings Minutes, 1918-1947, [partial] 1v. Transscripts (handwritten). Greek text.
Baptismal, Death, Wedding Registers, 1933-1968 [partial] 3v. Transcripts (handwritten). Greek text.
Inquiries invited: Rev. Dennis Michelis.

St. Demetrios (Hellenic Orthodox Community of Astoria, St. Demetrios), Astoria, Long Island City, New York. Parish Records, Baptismal, Marriage and Death Dating Back to 1934.
Inquiries invited: Rev. Dr. John A. Poulos.

Folklore Archives, Department of English, Wayne State University. Holdings: Extensive folklore material in many areas of folklore including about 45 pieces dealing with Modern Greek Folklore in the United States. Most of the material was obtained from foreign born Greeks or Americans of Greek descent.

Inquiries invited: Dr. Ellen Steckert, Director.

"Two Kolyva Recipes" obtained from Informants in Lancaster, Pennsylvania, and Warren, Ohio. Transcripts (Typewritten and handwritten) January, 1969. Includes information on informants and collector.

(BIF)

Agnew, Spiro. Biographical Materials Obtained from the Baltimore Sun Newspaper.

PLF (E-81)

St. Haralambos Greek Orthodox Church, Canton, Ohio.

Parish Minutes, n.d.

Parish Registers, n.d.

Inquiries invited: Rev. Nicholas C. Manikas.

Helicon Club. Collection of documents and other papers relating to the formation and activities of the Helicon Club. The Helicon Club is the Greek Students Association of America founded by Aristide Phoutrides ca. 1910-. Educ. 5329.222* In Harvard University Library.

Helicon, Inc. (Greek Students Association Founded by Aristide Phoutrides, Cambridge, Massachusetts, ca. 1910.) Correspondence 1939-1942. Fraternal Membership Lists (Various New England Colleges) ca. 1939. Part of N. Culolias Papers. Notebook H-VI, Box 4/5, Nicholas C. Culolias Papers.

Holy Trinity Archdiocesan Greek Cathedral, New York, New York. Parish Records, Baptismal, Marriage, Deaths from 1892+.

Inquiries invited:

Mr. Ernest A. Villas, Director

Department of Laity-Youth, Greek Orthodox Archdiocese of North and South America

777 United Nations Plaza, New York, New York

Lancaster County, Prothonotary's Office, Lancaster, Pennsylvania. Naturalization Docket, 1898-1966, Common Pleas. Transcripts (handwritten) of Greek aliens.

Includes: Name of Greek alien; residence; date of filing declaration intention; place, filing petition; disposition; granted or refused; attorney.

PLF (BIF)

Rankin, Lois. Papers, ca. 1933. Transcripts (handwritten and typewritten) dealing with Greeks in Detroit. One folder in John Burton Collection, Detroit Public Library.

RESEARCH IN PROGRESS

American Institutes for Research
Institutes for Research in Education
P. O. Box 1113, Palo Alto, Calif. 94302
1791 Arastradero Road, Palo Alto

Assumption of the Blessed Virgin
Springfield, Ohio
> Twenty-fifth Anniversary Yearbook will be available in 1970.
> Inquiries invited: Rev. Photios Tomarakos

International Institute of Metropolitan Detroit
Peoples of Detroit   Project
> Inquiries invited:
> Dr. Florence Cassidy, Director
> Survey of Ethnic & Parish Organizations in Detroit Michigan, 1968.

Pennsylvania Historical & Museum Commission
> The Ethnic Culture Survey dealing with the gathering of folk material not only of Greeks in Pennsylvania but also many other ethnic groups in Pennsylvania.

> Inquiries invited:
> Henry Glassie, State Folklorist
> Pennsylvania Historical & Museum Comm.
> Harrisburg, Pennsylvania

Rothschild, Constantina Safilios
> Survey of Sociologists who have completed or are working on Greek-Americans, 1968.
> Merrill-Palmer Institute, Detroit, Mich.

St. Sophia Greek Orthodox Church, Albany, New York
> Consecration Album available in May, 1969.
> Inquiries invited: Rev. Alexander Lendis

Spiegel, John P.

"Cultural Values and Mental Health in Greek-American Families."
1963, 1966.
Veterans Administration Hospital
Brockton, Mass.
Science Information Exchange Number
ZO 19525,ZO19,525 C3.   2 p. Xerox.

INDEX

Only authors, parish names (with location) and serial titles are indexed. Miscellaneous items are indexed at the end. The references are to the page number(s).

95

Greek-American Progressive
Association, 62
Greek-American Review, 60
The Greek Blue Book, 55
Greek News—Chicago, 60
Greek News—Los Angeles, 60
Greek Orhtodox Archdiocese of North
and South America:
Department of Education, 85
Department of Laity, 86
Department of Press and
Information, 86
Hellenic College, 86
Holy Cross Theological School, 87
Office of Publication, 87
St. Basil's Academy, 85
Greek Orthodox Community—Hunts-
ville, Alabama, 62
Greek Orthodox Theological Review,
57
Greek Orthodox Youth of America,
62, 63
G.O.Y.A Bulletin, 57
Greek Press, 57
Greek Review, 59
Greek Republican Club, Boston,
Massachusetts, 63
Green, Arnold W., 32
Grigorieff, D., 45
Grossberg, Elmer, 39

Halley, Hellen, 49
Hamilton, A., 35
Hammond, Peter, 44
Harris, Jennie E., 32
Hartley, H., 30
Helicon Club, 90
Helicon, Inc., 90
Hellenic Association of Boston, 63
Hellenic Chronicle, 57
Hellenic Free Press, 57
Hellenic News, 57
Hellenic Renaissance, 60
Hellenic Review & Economics. . ., 57
*Hellenic Review & International
Report*, 57
Hellenic Spectator, 30, 60
Helmis, George N., 54
Historical Records Survey, 48
Holbrook, Agnes Sinclair, 26
Hole, Jonathan A., 36
Holy Cross Greek Orthodox Church—
Belmont, California, 75
Holy Cross Greek Orthodox Church—
Pittsburgh, Pennsylvania, 75

Holy Mother of God Greek Orthodox
Church—Tallahasee, Florida, 76
Holy Transfiguration Monastery, 40,
47, 76
Holy Trinity and St. John the Divine
—Jackson, Mississippi, 78
Holy Trinity Archdiocesan Greek
Cathedral—New York, New York,
90
Holy Trinity Greek Orthodox Church
—Charleston, South Carolina, 76
Holy Trinity Greek Orthodox Church
—Chicago, Illinois, 77
Holy Trinity Greek Orthodox Church
—Concord, New Hampshire, 77
Holy Trinity Greek Orthodox Church
—Fond Du Lac, Wisconsin, 77
Holy Trinity Greek Orthodox Church
—Holyoke, Massachusetts, 77
Holy Trinity Greek Orthodox Church
—Lewistown, Maine, 77
Holy Trinity Greek Orthodox Church
—Orlando, Florida, 78
Holy Trinity Greek Orthodox Church
—Steubenville, Ohio, 78
Holy Trinity Greek Orthodox Church
—Westfeild, New Jersey, 78
Holy Trinity Greek Orthodox Church
—Wilmington, Delaware, 78
Hunt, Milton B., 27

Institute of Texan Cultures, 52
International Institute of Metropolitan Detroit, 92

Jackson, Maria, 49
Janetis, Elias, 22
Joachim, K. K., 43
Johnstone, John, 47

Kallimachos, Demetrios, 36
Kalymhos Society, 63
Kamal, Ahmad, 39
Kantor, MacKinley, 39
Katsanevas, Mike, 35
Kazan, Elia, 41
Keker, Joan, 48
Kerr, Annie Barclay, 39
Key, A., 31
Kimbrough, Emily, 41
Kimissis, Theotokou,—Racine,
Wisconsin, 80
Kiriazis, James W., 51
Kollias, Sephes G., 22, 24
Kontargyres, Theodoros N., 24